On
Law and Power

Sources in Early Modern Economics, Ethics, and Law

General Editors

Jordan J. Ballor, Acton Institute
Stephen J. Grabill, Acton Institute

The disciplines of economics, ethics, and law cannot be detached from a historical background that was; it is increasingly recognized, religious in nature. Economists Adam Smith and Léon Walras drew on the work of sixteenth- and seventeenth-century Spanish theologians who strove to understand the process of exchange and trade in order to better articulate subjective value, a dynamic theory of money, the role of the merchant, and the concept of marginal utility. Likewise, political theorists John Neville Figgis and Otto von Gierke drew on the work of sixteenth- and seventeenth-century Dutch, Swiss, German, and Spanish jurists and ethicists who articulated concepts that laid the foundation for federalist political structures, constitutionalism, popular sovereignty, natural-law jurisprudence, and limited government in the Western legal tradition. After a long period in which economics, ethics, and law became detached from theology, many economists, legal scholars, political theorists, and theologians now see the benefit of studying early modern economic, ethical, and legal texts in their full cultural, often religious, context. This series, *Sources in Early Modern Economics, Ethics, and Law*, provides first-ever English translations and editions of some of the most formative but previously inaccessible texts that shaped the disciplines of economics, ethics, and law in the early modern era and beyond. These inexpensive translations of seminal texts will make substantive contributions to contemporary interdisciplinary discussion.

ON
Law and Power

Johannes Althusius

Translated by Jeffrey J. Veenstra

Introductions by Stephen J. Grabill and John Witte, Jr.

CLP Academic
GRAND RAPIDS · MICHIGAN

Refo500

On Law and Power

Translated by Jeffrey J. Veenstra

Cover image: Emden (Lower Saxony, Germany), new church ("Neue Kirche"), June 2005
Source: Tim Schredder, licensed under the Creative Commons Attribution 3.0 Unported license
URL: wikimedia.org/wiki/File:Emden_Neue_Kirche.jpg
Inset photo: Wikimedia Commons (http://commons.wikimedia.org/wiki/File:JohannesAlthusius.png)

ISBN: 978-1-938948-59-6

Christian's Library Press

An imprint of the Acton Institute for the Study of Religion & Liberty

98 E. Fulton
Grand Rapids, Michigan 49503
Phone: 616.454.3080
Fax: 616.454.9454
www.clpress.com

Interior composition by Judy Schafer
Cover design by Peter Ho
Editorial assistance by Joe Carter, Andrew M. McGinnis, and Dylan Pahman

Printed in the United States of America

Contents

Sources in Early Modern Economics, Ethics, and Law

Series Introduction

Jordan J. Ballor
Stephen J. Grabill

For the same underlying reasons that moral theology is held in disrepute by many Western intellectuals, modern economists tend to glibly dismiss or even simply ignore the economic ideas of the scholastics, whether those of the twelfth or the seventeenth century. For many intellectuals nowadays, moral theology has come to signify a passé form of religious thinking that embraces irrationality and dogmatism, and economic historians—along with notable astrophysicists, geneticists, paleontologists, political analysts, philosophers, and ethicists—have all espoused this line of thought. Among the latter, in particular, the identification of scholastic economics (or the "canonical concept of market behavior," as it is sometimes called) with Aristotelian metaphysics and ecclesiastical authority has made modern economic professionals reticent or, at the very least unreceptive, to acknowledging any sophisticated analytical contribution to monetary and value theory by the Schoolmen or the Doctors—their sixteenth- and seventeenth-century heirs.

The severing of economic ideas from their original historical and metaphysical contexts becomes especially pronounced in the contemporary debate over the prehistory of economics. Invariably, most mainstream economic historians locate the birth of modern economics in Adam Smith, the mercantilists, and the physiocrats. For historian of economics Mark Blaug, the prehistory of economics begins with the seventeenth-century mercantilists and not, as the revisionists insist, with either the ancient Greeks or the medieval scholastics. He coins the term *pre-Adamite economics* to methodologically define and restrict the era of prehistory to Smith's immediate and direct historical precursors: the seventeenth-century mercantilists, the physiocrats, and the British free-trade writers of the eighteenth century.

The broader question of whether the prehistory of economics should start in the thirteenth century or much earlier is, in Blaug's estimation, "an afterthought."[1] An afterthought, we might infer, which could presumably surface information that would challenge positivist assumptions about human behavior and social cohesion and one that will yield few, if any, new insights into quantitative methods and models. Where the scholastics analyzed economic and commercial transactions as either ethical or legal matters involving the application of natural law to civil contracts, "it was the mercantilists," contends Blaug, "who, long before Adam Smith, broke with the canonical conception of market behavior as a moral problem and fashioned the concept of 'economic man.'" These mercantilists

> believed in the direct power of self-interest and in matters of domestic economic policy came near to advocating laissez-faire. Adam Smith was not the first to have confidence in the workings of the 'invisible hand.' Nor is it necessary to

1. Mark Blaug, *Economic Theory in Retrospect*, 5th ed. (Cambridge: Cambridge University Press, 1997), 29.

> appeal to scholastic influences to account for his grasp of the determination of prices by demand and supply.[2]

Regardless of whether it is necessary to appeal to scholastic influences to explain how Smith, in particular, understood price and value to be determined, such a determination does not speak to the wider issue of whether such seminal figures in the history of economics as Bernardo Davanzati (1529–1606), Hugo Grotius (1583–1645), Samuel von Pufendorf (1632–1694), Gershom Carmichael (1672–1729), Francis Hutcheson (1694–1746), Jean-Jacques Burlamaqui (1694–1748), Adam Ferguson (1723–1816), Ferdinando Galiani (1728–1787), Auguste Walras (1801–1866), and Léon Walras (1834–1910) were influenced by scholastic treatments of price and value. Neither does this judgment determine, for that matter, whether Smith's entire system of thought remains intelligible if the role he assigns to teleology, final causes, divine design, and virtue is disregarded as merely ornamental.[3] In this wider respect, therefore, the modern quibble over scholastic influences in Smith is a red herring because, as Langholm attests, it sidesteps serious historical investigation into the continuities and discontinuities between scholastic and modern economic ideas.[4] Furthermore, it also has the convenient side effect of

2. Blaug, *Economic Theory in Retrospect*, 31.

3. See James E. Alvey, "The Secret, Natural Theological Foundation of Adam Smith's Work," *Journal of Markets & Morality* 7, no. 2 (Fall 2004): 335–61. See also Paul Oslington, ed., *Adam Smith as Theologian* (New York: Routledge, 2011).

4. "From an analytical and terminological point of view," writes Langholm, "there is much of scholastic teaching that can be seen to have survived into modern economics. This is not surprising, since (at least if this observation is limited to our Western civilization) it was in the high Middle Ages that the foundations were laid for the kind of systematic reasoning about social relationships that has run on continually to the present day. Sometimes, as in the case of the fairness of the market price, it was deemed pertinent above to point out a subtle shift in the moral basis that supported an apparently unaltered doctrine. Elsewhere, where doctrines

downplaying the importance of teleology and natural theology in the thought of Smith himself and other seventeenth-, eighteenth-, and nineteenth-century political economists.

By methodologically constricting the prehistory of economics to the mercantilists and the physiocrats, as positivist historiographers commend, economic history congeals around such characteristically "modern" concerns as the concept of "economic man," self-interest, and the emancipation of economics from the so-called canonical concept of market behavior. This arbitrary limitation of which ideas and which people carry weight in economic history only serves to bolster twentieth-century positivist assumptions, particularly those of value neutrality and *homo economicus*, the assumption that humans act as rational and self-interested agents who desire wealth, avoid unnecessary labor, and seek to order their decision making exclusively around those goals. In the end, the modern reduction of the prehistory of economics to the seventeenth-century mercantilists can be put in the form of an Occam's razor-like question: Why appeal to scholastic influences to illumine modern notions of money,

---

have changed as radically as in the case of lending at interest, the scholastics can still be credited with posing the terms of an ongoing argument. Therefore, it would seem that much of the old vessel remained to receive new content. The question is how completely it was ever emptied of the ferment prepared for it in the medieval schools. This subject requires a book rather than a few lines. In fact, it has been the subject of many books, some of them provoked or inspired by Max Weber's ideas about religion and capitalism. For simplicity, let us recall that scholastic economics rested on three intellectual traditions. The first support was the tradition of the Bible and the Church Fathers with its emphasis on individual duty. The second was the tradition of the recently rediscovered Roman law with its emphasis on individual rights. The two traditions were made to balance briefly and precariously in the Thomist synthesis by means of a third support in Aristotelian social philosophy." See Odd Langholm, "Scholastic Economics," in *Pre-Classical Economic Thought: From the Greeks to the Scottish Enlightenment*, ed. S. Todd Lowry (Boston/Dordrecht/Lancaster: Kluwer Academic Publishers, 1987), 132–33.

value, and price when all the basic elements of classical economics are already embedded in mercantilism?

The most straightforward reply is that seminal ideas, which include revolutionary economic ideas, never develop in intellectual, historical, religious, philosophical, or geographical vacuums. "Enlightened," secular reaction to the medieval Church's temporal jurisdiction and to theology's intellectual hegemony as the queen of the sciences has created a modern milieu in which scholars are no longer even aware of the historical influence that fundamental Christian doctrines have exerted in Western culture and university life.[5] From very early times, Christian theologians assumed that the application of patterns of discursive reasoning (as in the scholastic method, which was a method instituted by medieval Christian theologians and adapted and applied for subsequent centuries) could yield an increasingly accurate understanding not only of God's word and moral will but also of the created order itself.

Thus the systematic application of reason to a variety of intellectual undertakings, including economic problems, was not the invention of the Enlightenment. Rather, the application of reason within a coherent intellectual framework is the legacy of Christian scholasticism—the method of the medieval and early modern schools. The application of this scholastic method led to increased understanding of the world and human affairs, and spurred efforts to formulate logical explanations of regular occurrences in nature. "All things possess order amongst themselves: this order is the form that makes the world resemble God," wrote Dante in the *Divine Comedy*.[6] It can be argued that the specific application of scholastic method to economic

---

5. See Chris L. Firestone and Nathan Jacobs, eds., *The Persistence of the Sacred in Modern Thought* (Notre Dame: University of Notre Dame Press, 2012).

6. Dante, *Paradise*, trans. Anthony Esolen (New York: Modern Library, 2004), 1:103–5, p. 9.

problems became the seedbed for innovative ideas that, after much dialectical refinement, came to shape the world of modern economics. The truth of this statement does not rest on modernity's own understanding of its birth, development, or future trajectory but rather on the demonstrable "internal interconnections and affinities among ideas, their dynamism or 'particular go' (Lovejoy's phrase), and the logical pressures they are capable of exerting on the minds of those that think them."[7]

Assent to this claim, however, will require the positivist historian to reconsider not only the relationship between metaphysical schemata and intellectual traditions, which, in turn, will require an acknowledgement of the indispensable role of theological doctrines in the history of ideas,[8] but it will also require an admission that the recent detachment of economics from morality is itself a novelty, an aberration from a long-standing tradition within political economy itself.[9] In Alvey's judgment,

7. Francis Oakley, *Natural Law, Laws of Nature, Natural Rights: Continuity and Discontinuity in the History of Ideas* (New York and London: Continuum, 2005), 9.

8. See Oakley, *Natural Law, Laws of Nature, Natural Rights*, 13–34. See also the various essays in Oakley's *Politics and Eternity: Studies in the History of Medieval and Early-Modern Political Thought* (Leiden: Brill, 1999); Oakley, *Omnipotence, Covenant, and Order: An Excursion in the History of Ideas from Abelard to Leibniz* (Ithaca: Cornell University Press, 1984); Oakley, *Kingship: The Politics of Enchantment* (Oxford: Blackwell Publishing, 2006); and William J. Courtenay, *Covenant and Causality in Medieval Thought: Studies in Philosophy, Theology, and Economic Practice* (London: Variorum Reprints, 1984).

9. Broadly, on the historical constriction and positivism of contemporary economic thinking, see John D. Mueller, *Redeeming Economics: Rediscovering the Missing Element* (Wilmington, DE: ISI Books, 2010). See also Jeffrey T. Young, *Economics as a Moral Science: The Political Economy of Adam Smith* (Cheltenham, UK: Edward Elgar, 1997); James Alvey, "A Short History of Economics as a Moral Science," *Journal of Markets & Morality* 2, no. 1 (Spring 1999): 53–73; Ricardo F. Crespo, "Is Economics a Moral Science?," *Journal of Markets & Morality* 1, no. 2 (Fall 1998): 201–11; Peter J. Boettke, "Is Economics a Moral Science? A Response to Ricardo F. Crespo,"

> There are two major reasons why economics has become detached from moral concerns. First, the natural sciences came to be seen as successful, and the attempt was made to emulate that success in economics by applying natural science methods, including mathematics, to economic phenomena. Second, the self-styled economic science came to adopt positivism, which ruled out moral issues from science itself.[10]

It is the latter recognition, perhaps more than any other, that squares the revisionists off against the positivists in the debate over the prehistory of economics.

When the positivistic bias begins to be put aside and we look anew at works from earlier periods, we find the early modern era to be a rich source of intellectual ferment on economic, ethical, and legal and political topics. In the sixteenth and early seventeenth centuries, a small but influential group of theologians and jurists centered in Spain attempted to synthesize the Roman legal texts with Aristotelian and Thomistic moral philosophy. The movement began with the revival of Thomistic philosophy in Paris, where, as Camacho recounts, "Pierre Crockaert underwent an intellectual conversion from nominalist philosophy to the philosophy of Thomas Aquinas."[11]

Shortly before 1225, the year of Aquinas' birth, Aristotle's works on metaphysics, physics, politics, and ethics became available in the West, and, within the span of a generation, Aristotelianism,

---

Journal of Markets & Morality 1, no. 2 (Fall 1998): 212–19; and Crespo, "Is Economics a Moral Science? A Response to Peter J. Boettke," *Journal of Markets & Morality* 1, no. 2 (Fall 1998): 220–25; Jeffrey T. Young, *Economics as a Moral Science: The Political Economy of Adam Smith* (Cheltenham, UK: Edward Elgar, 1997).

10. Alvey, "A Short History of Economics as a Moral Science," 53.

11. Francisco Gómez Camacho, "Later Scholastics: Spanish Economic Thought in the Sixteenth and Seventeenth Centuries," in *Ancient and Medieval Economic Ideas and Concepts of Social Justice*, ed. S. Todd Lowry and Barry Gordon (Leiden and New York: Brill, 1998), 503.

which had been brought to Europe by Arabic scholars, would be a serious contender in medieval thought. Thomas sought a rapprochement between the Greek philosophical tradition that Aristotle represented and the Christian divine ideas tradition articulated by the likes of Augustine, pseudo-Dionysius, and Bonaventure. In 1512, Crockaert published his commentary on the last part of Thomas' *Summa theologica* with the help of a student, Francisco de Vitoria (ca. 1483–1546).[12]

Approximately two hundred years before Thomas was born, the *Corpus iuris civilis* of Justinian had been rediscovered and had become the object of academic disputation. However, the traditions of Roman law and Aristotelian and Thomistic philosophy existed in relative isolation from one other, at least until the early sixteenth century in Spain. "In the sixteenth and early seventeenth centuries," states Camacho, "a synthesis was finally achieved by that group of theologians and jurists known to historians of law as the 'late scholastics' or the 'Spanish natural law school.'"[13] Schumpeter concurs with this judgment and adds, "It is within their systems of moral theology and law that economics gained definite if not separate existence, and it is they who come nearer than does any other group to having been the 'founders' of scientific economics."[14] The Salamancans in particular, writes Moss,

12. Camacho, "Later Scholastics: Spanish Economic Thought in the Sixteenth and Seventeenth Centuries," 503.

13. Camacho, "Later Scholastics: Spanish Economic Thought in the Sixteenth and Seventeenth Centuries," 503.

14. Joseph Schumpeter, *History of Economic Analysis*, ed. Elizabeth Booty Schumpeter (Oxford: Oxford University Press, 1954), 97: "And not only that it will appear, even, that the bases they laid for a serviceable and well-integrated body of analytic tools and propositions were sounder than was much subsequent work, in the sense that a considerable part of the economics of the later nineteenth century might have been developed from those bases more quickly and with less trouble than it actually cost

> were as interested in a general theory of how exchange rates between different currencies are formed as in explaining why a bill of exchange is worth more in one region of Spain than in another region. Was the agio or exchange premium evidence of usury and therefore immoral behavior on the part of merchants and traders, or rather something 'natural' governed by the basic laws of supply and demand?[15]

The case of this so-called School of Salamanca is just one example of the rich intellectual traditions that have far too often been ignored or downplayed by contemporary scholarship. The coherent intellectual framework of Christian scholasticism reverberates not only in the field of economics but also in the related areas of ethics and law. Thus, political theorists John Neville Figgis and Otto von Gierke drew on the work of a variety of sixteenth- and seventeenth-century Dutch, Swiss, German, and Spanish jurists and ethicists who articulated concepts that laid the foundation for federalist political structures, constitutionalism, popular sovereignty, natural-law jurisprudence, and limited government in the Western legal tradition.[16] The diversity and variety of relevant sources from this period is underscored by the contribution of Protestant scholars, who produced significant scholastic works as well as more occasional treatises. Much of the early Protestant thought on economics, ethics, and law attaches to their homiletical and exegetical work in addition to the achievements in systems of moral theology and philosophy. The Dutch

---

to develop it, and that some of that subsequent work was therefore in the nature of a time- and labor-consuming detour."

15. Laurence S. Moss, "Introduction," in *Economic Thought in Spain: Selected Essays of Marjorie Grice-Hutchinson*, ed. Laurence S. Moss and Christopher K. Ryan (Brookfield, VT: Edward Elgar, 1993), xv.

16. On Johannes Althusius in particular, see Otto von Gierke, *The Development of Political Theory*, trans. Bernard Freyd (New York: Howard Fertig, 1966), 70; and John Neville Figgis, *Studies of Political Thought: From Gerson to Grotius, 1414–1625* (Cambridge: Cambridge University Press, 1907), 175–85.

Reformed legal thinker Johannes Althusius (1563–1638) stands as a representative example in this regard, and his contributions to the development of Western legal and political traditions are becoming increasingly appreciated.[17] After a long period in which economics, ethics, and law became detached from theology, many economists, legal scholars, political theorists, and theologians now see the benefit of studying early modern economic, ethical, and legal texts in their full cultural, often religious, context.

The Sources in Early Modern Economics, Ethics, and Law series is the latest installment in the excavation of the mines of early modern theological thought on these topics. The aim of this series is to offer economists, intellectual historians, moral theologians, and graduate students in the fields of economics, economic ethics, economic history, banking history, political economy, and moral theology a useful and accessible collection of some of the most important early modern texts in the fields of economics, ethics, and law. Now, for the first time, the unabridged texts of works such as Martín de Azpilcueta's *Commentary on the Resolution of Money* (1556), Luis de Molina's *Treatise on Money* (1597), and Juan de Mariana's *Treatise on the Alteration of Money* (1609), as well as selections from larger works such as Johannes Althusius' *Dicaeologicae* (1617) and Girolamo Zanchi's *Omnium operum theologicorum* (1619) will be available as stand-alone volumes in English translation and in modern editions with scholarly annotations. We hope that the publication of these primary texts in a series of paperbacks will help to facilitate exploration of the continuities and discontinuities,

17. See, for instance, John Witte Jr., "A Demonstrative Theory of Natural Law: The Original Contribution of Johannes Althusius," in *Public Theology for a Global Society: Essays in Honor of Max L. Stackhouse*, ed. Deirdre King Hainsworth and Scott R. Paeth (Grand Rapids: Eerdmans, 2010), 21–36; and Thomas O. Hueglin, *Early Modern Concepts for a Late Medieval World: Althusius on Community and Federalism* (Waterloo, ON: Wilfrid Laurier University Press, 1999).

agreements and disagreements, innovations and ruptures among theological communities during the latter half of the sixteenth and the early seventeenth century.

The translations and modern editions (in conjunction with the introductions by leading authorities) will show the sophistication with which Christian thinkers from a variety of confessional and theological perspectives examined issues such as the role and responsibilities of the civil magistrates, the existence and efficacy of natural law, usury, and the ethics of moneylending, as well as the new process of using bills of exchange (*cambium per litteras*) to replace the cumbersome and dangerous transportation of metallic coins between commercial fairs, which led not only to new scholastic insights on interest, credit, and international trade but also to a much more comprehensive analysis of monetary exchange and banking practices than had been undertaken before. The texts will also address the questions as particular as why the same currency was worth more in one region than another area's currency, and, moreover, why the rate of exchange fluctuated between one area and the next. These moral and economic concerns, along with many others, will be addressed in detail throughout the course of the series by some of the leading, and heretofore underappreciated, authorities from the early modern era.

Althusius in Context: A Biographical and Historical Introduction

Stephen J. Grabill

Johannes Althusius, whose surname appears variously as Althus, Althusen, or Althaus, was born in 1557 at Diedenshausen, a village in the countship of Witgenstein-Berleburg.[1] Very little

1. In the interest of brevity, I have largely followed the overviews of Althusius's life found in Otto von Gierke's *The Development of Political Theory*, trans. Bernard Freyd (New York: Howard Fertig, 1966), 19–21; and in Frederick S. Carney, "Translator's Introduction," in *Politica: An Abridged Translation of Politics Methodically Set Forth and Illustrated with Sacred and Profane Examples*, ed. and trans. Frederick S. Carney (Indianapolis: Liberty Fund, 1995), xi–xii.

A longer, fuller treatment of his life can be found in Carl Joachim Friedrich's introduction to the *Politica Methodice Digesta of Johannes Althusius (Althaus)* (Cambridge, MA: Harvard University Press, 1932; New York: Arno Press, 1979), xxiii–xli; Thomas O. Hueglin, *Early Modern Concepts for a Late Modern World: Althusius on Community and Federalism* (Waterloo, Ont.: Wilfrid Laurier University Press, 1999), 29–41; and Corrado Malandrino, "Il *Syndikat* di Johannes Althusius a Emden: La ricerca," *Pensiero Politico* 28, no. 3 (1995): 359–83. This article endeavors to correct some of the weaknesses in Heinz Werner Antholz's *Die politische Wirksamkeit des Johannes Althusius in Emden* (Aurich: Abhandlungen und Vorträge zur Geschichte Ostfrieslands, 1955), the only major work on the subject.

is known for certain about his parents, his youth, or his early course of studies. He appeared at Cologne in 1581, where he apparently studied the writings of Aristotle. At some point prior to obtaining his doctorate, Althusius also studied law at Geneva with Denis Godefroy (1549–1622), the renowned legal scholar who published the first complete edition of Roman Civil Law in 1583.[2] Althusius received his doctorate in both civil and canon law at Basel in 1586. Astonishingly, he published his first book *Jurisprudentiae Romanae*, which was a systematic treatise on Roman law based on the Godefroy edition, during the same year. While at Basel, he lived for a time in the home of Johannes Grynaeus (1540–1617), with whom he studied Reformed theology, and thereafter maintained a lifelong correspondence.

In 1586, he accepted a call to teach in the law faculty in the Reformed Academy at Herborn. The Academy, which had been founded only two years earlier by Count John VI of Nassau-Dillenburg (1535–1606), became immediately successful and attracted an international student body. Its first rector was Caspar Olevianus (1536–1587), the coauthor with Zacharias Ursinus (1534–1583) of the Heidelberg Catechism.[3] As the first professor of law at Herborn, Althusius began lecturing on Justinian's *Institutes*, but his teaching interests soon shifted to the science of public law, or what is now political science. In 1589, he became a member of the count's Chancery at Dillenburg and later became councilor to the count (1595).[4] After studying theology

2. Carney, "Translator's Introduction," xi.

3. Carney, "Translator's Introduction," xi.

4. The internationally esteemed legal historian Harold Berman makes a fascinating point about the dramatic change that occurred in the political role of the jurist during the sixteenth century: "Together with these rather obvious links between the new legal science and the new political order in Protestant principalities, there existed a more subtle link: the exaltation of the political role of the legal scholar. In pre-Reformation Europe as well, legal scholars had played an important role as advisors to popes, emperors, and kings. They also had sometimes been asked by judges to

for a time in Heidelberg,[5] Althusius was made rector of the Academy in 1597. His second book, a volume on ethics titled *Civilis conversationis libri duo*, was published in 1601. The most notable achievement of his tenure at Herborn was the publication in 1603 of the *Politica methodice digesta & exemplis sacris & profanis illustrata*, a work that received immediate and widespread attention.

Even though Althusius had already begun to establish a scholarly reputation with his first and second books, it was the *Politica* that seems to have been instrumental in securing for him an attractive offer to become syndic of Emden in Friesland. Althusius assumed his duties in 1604 and led the city's legal and political

---

decide cases. Never before, however, had legal scholars been recruited as councilors and judges so systematically and on such a large scale as in the sixteenth-century German Protestant principalities. This was due in part, of course, to purely political factors; but it was also due in part to the character of the new legal science, which was so intellectually complex and intricate as to require professorial expertise to articulate and elucidate it." See Harold J. Berman, *Law and Revolution, II: The Impact of the Protestant Reformations on the Western Legal Tradition* (Cambridge, MA: Harvard University Press, 2003), 128.

5. Althusius's time in Heidelberg reading and interacting with the Reformed faculty was formative on his intellectual development. According to Carney, "The churchly writings of John Calvin, Jerome Zanchius, Benedict Aretius, and Zachary Ursinus are the major sources for Althusius' exposition of the ecclesiastical order in both the province and the commonwealth. Zanchius' extensive discussion of law in his *De redemptione* contributes more than anything else to Althusius' understanding of the relation of the Decalogue to natural law, and of both to the proper laws of various nations. Then there are special topics on which Althusius finds his theological colleagues to be helpful, such as Peter Martyr's discussion of war" (Carney, "Translator's Introduction," xxvii). Zanchi taught at Heidelberg from the late 1560s to the mid-1570s, during which he published his massive treatise on law (*De redemptione*). For more on Zanchi's influence on Althusius, see Stephen J. Grabill, "Introduction," in *On the Law in General*, by Girolamo Zanchi, trans. Jeffrey J. Veenstra (Grand Rapids: CLP Academic, 2012), xix–xxviii; and Grabill, *Rediscovering the Natural Law in Reformed Theological Ethics* (Grand Rapids: Eerdmans, 2006), 132–42.

affairs without interruption until his death in 1638. During his lengthy term of service, he engaged in strategic diplomatic missions with the territorial authorities to assist Emden in achieving independent statehood, he also developed and maintained a municipal constitution, and kept up with his literary pursuits. He published two new and enlarged editions of the *Politica* (1610 and 1614), and also wrote the *Dicaeologicae* (1617), a work in which he systematized the entire body of existing law and coordinated it with Roman and Jewish civil law. In 1617, Althusius was elected elder of the church of Emden, and was highly esteemed by the Reformed clergy under the leadership of Menso Alting (1541–1612). "There is a sense in which [Althusius's] two functions of syndic and elder, coupled with capacities for leadership and hard work," observes Carney, "enabled him to coordinate the civil and ecclesiastical jurisdictions of the city, and thus to exercise somewhat the same kind of influence in Emden as Calvin did in Geneva."[6]

Johannes Althusius: Political Theorist and Jurist

Until Otto von Gierke's (1841–1921) rediscovery of Althusius in the 1880s, few political theorists and jurists, and even fewer theologians, had any substantive appreciation for Althusius's contribution to either the Western political canon or the Western legal tradition. One possible explanation for the rather slow reception of Althusius among twentieth-century scholars, at least until recently, is that prior to Frederick Carney's 1964 translation there had been no published translation of a substantial portion of the *Politica* in any vernacular language.[7] This state of affairs has

6. Carney, "Translator's Introduction," xii.

7. Johannes Althusius, *Politics*, trans. Frederick S. Carney (Boston: Beacon, 1964). In its 1995 edition, Liberty Fund reprinted this earlier translation and added a lengthy introduction by Carney, a foreword by Daniel Elazar, a chapter on the literary sources that Althusius refers to in the translation,

changed in the last few years. In 2003, an unabridged translation of the *Politica* into German was published,[8] leaving the rest of Althusius's Latin corpus untranslated, the only exception being the selections from the *Dicaeologicae* in the present volume that previously appeared in the *Journal of Markets & Morality* and now, in corrected and updated form, in the present volume for the first time in English translation.[9] Another factor contributing to his relative obscurity, however, is less benign: Althusius was the focus of a maelstrom of criticism from all sides by seventeenth-century polemicists, including Henning Arnisaeus (d. 1636) and Hugo Grotius (1583–1645). From the mid-seventeenth century onward, he was routinely attacked by Hermann Conring (1606–1681), Naamann Bensen (1622–1659), Peter Gartz (fl. 1640), Johann Heinrich Boecler (1611–1672), and Ulrich Huber (1636–1694) who insisted that the *Politica* was "a book worthy of the flames," "the most noxious fruit of Monarcho-machism," "the dogma of popular sovereignty a product of Presbyterian error," and its author "the seditious architect of disorder."[10]

It should hardly be surprising that the *Politica* would occasion such searing indictments, for it vigorously defended the local autonomies of the old plural order of guilds, estates, and cities against the rise of territorial absolutism and those early apologists of the modern unitary nation state such as Jean Bodin (1520–1596) and Thomas Hobbes (1588–1679). Furthermore, in later editions of the *Politica*, Althusius urged readers to follow closely the logic of the arguments presented therein because they

---

a note on the Liberty Fund edition, a collation of this translation with the 1614 edition, and a register of Althusius's writings.

8. Johannes Althusius, *Politik*, ed. Dieter Wyduckel, trans. Heinrich Janssen (Berlin: Duncker and Humblot, 2003).

9. *Journal of Markets & Morality* 9, no. 2 (2006): 429–83. The selections are translated from the second edition, revised, of the *Dicaeologicae*, which was published in Frankfurt in 1649 by the Heirs of Christophorus Corvinus. This edition of the *Dicaeologicae* was reprinted by Scientia (Aalen) in 1967.

10. Gierke, *The Development of Political Theory*, 16–18.

provided theoretical justification for the Dutch revolt from Spain. That much is clear from the dedication of the book (second and third editions) to the Estates of Frisia, which he praised for their role in resisting the king of Spain and in fearlessly proclaiming the right of sovereignty "to reside in the association of the multitude and the people of the individual provinces."[11] Needless to say, the *Politica* was one of the most widely read and, by some, the most despised book of its day.

Besides the *Politica*, Althusius wrote a series of treatises in jurisprudence, of which two undertook a systematic treatment of civil law. The first of these appeared in 1586 at Basel under the title: *Jurisprudentiae Romanae libri duo ad leges methodi Rameae conformati et tabellis illustrati*. This book was widely used as a legal textbook and went through several editions. It was later completely revised and published (at Herborn in 1617 and at Frankfurt in 1618 and 1649) as *Dicaeologicae libri tres, totum et universum jus, quo utimur, methodice complectentes, cum parallelis hujus et Judaici juris, tabulisque insertis atque Indice triplici*. The *Dicaeologicae* was an immense work (792 Latin folio pages) that sought to construct a single comprehensive juridical system by collating the Decalogue, Jewish law, Roman law, and various streams of European customary law. In the preface to the *Dicaeologicae*, Althusius explains that the *Jurisprudentiae* "has been praised and attacked at different times in different places contrary to my thoughts and anticipations." In fact, "learned and eminent men have advised me a number of times to recall that treatise so that I might iron out and explain more fully what I expressed rather succinctly, briefly, and obscurely. Diligently have I obeyed my advisors and whatever leisure time I have had away from my duties and obligation to the state I devoted to this concern and pursuit. These earlier concerns have produced a

11. Johannes Althusius, "Preface to the 1614 edition," in *Politica*, ed. and trans. Frederick S. Carney (Indianapolis: Liberty Fund, 1995), 14.

work that is almost completely new and is, in fact, different in many ways from the previous one."[12]

The *Dicaeologicae* was Althusius's principal juridical work and evidences the "method" of legal systematization initiated at Wittenberg by Johann Apel (1486–1536) and Konrad Lagus (ca. 1499–1546). The new legal science pioneered in the works of Apel, Lagus, Nicolas Vigelius (1529–1600), and other early and middle sixteenth-century German Protestant jurists was strongly influenced by the topical method of the Reformer Philipp Melanchthon (1497–1560) and developed over the next two centuries by jurists throughout Europe, both Roman Catholic and Protestant. In Harold Berman's estimation, Johannes Althusius and Nicolas Vigelius are "among the most prominent German legal 'methodists' of the latter part of the sixteenth century."[13] The new legal science differed from the earlier legal sciences "in its use of topical method to analyze and synthesize law as a whole as well as to analyze and synthesize the various systems of law that prevailed in Europe—Roman, canon, royal, feudal, mercantile."[14] It was this legal science, above all, contend Berman and Reid, "that constituted the basis of the new European *jus commune* of the sixteenth to eighteenth centuries. The legal scholars who developed it formed a pan-European class of jurists, a *Juristenstand*, who wrote not only for their respective countrymen but also, and sometimes primarily, for each other."[15]

Finally, for the sake of completeness in our survey of Althusius's corpus, we should mention that he also wrote a system of practical ethics, which his cousin Philipp Althusius published

12. See pages 3–4.

13. Berman, *Law and Revolution, II*, 124.

14. Harold J. Berman and Charles J. Reid Jr., "Roman Law in Europe and the *Jus Commune*: A Historical Overview with Emphasis on the New Legal Science of the Sixteenth Century," *Syracuse Journal of International Law and Commerce* 20 (1994): 26.

15. Berman and Reid, "Roman Law in Europe and the *Jus Commune*," 26.

under the title: *Joh. Althusii V. Cl. Civilis conversationis libri duo, methodice digesti et exemplis sacris et profanis passim illustrati* at Hanau in 1601 (2nd ed. 1611).[16]

The Modern, Interdisciplinary Renaissance in Althusius Studies

As mentioned above, the modern resurgence of interest in Althusius began with the nineteenth-century German jurist and historian Otto von Gierke.[17] Gierke recovered Althusius from two centuries of relative obscurity and attributed to the *Politica* the distinction of making one of the pivotal contributions to Western political thought. He saw in Althusius a seminal thinker who was enabled by an exceptional education in law, theology, politics, and history to develop a political theory that served as a capstone of medieval social thought and a precursor to modern political ideas.[18] The chief feature of this theory, Gierke thought, was its federalist structure, which he understood to result from an admixture of contractual and natural-law principles. Althusius's main contribution, in Gierke's words, was "to give logical unity to the federal ideas that simmered in the ecclesiastical and political circles in which he lived, and to construct an audacious system of

16. Gierke, *The Development of Political Theory*, 21–22.

17. Otto Friedrich von Gierke taught law at the universities of Berlin, Breslau, and Heidelberg throughout his long and distinguished career. His chief works were: *Das deutsche Genossenschaftsrecht*, 4 vols. (Berlin: Weidmann, 1868–1913), of which *Natural Law and the Theory of Society, 1500–1800*, trans. Ernest Barker (Cambridge: Cambridge University Press, 1950) is a translation of five subsections of the fourth volume; *Johannes Althusius und die Entwicklung der naturrechtlichen Staatstheorien: zugleich ein Beitrag zur Geschichte der Rechtssystematik*, 5th ed. (Aalen: Scientia, 1958), which was translated into English as *The Development of Political Theory* but first appeared as the third volume in the series above; and *Deutsches privatrecht*, 3 vols. (Leipzig: Duncker and Humblot, 1895–1917).

18. Carney, "Translator's Introduction," ix.

thought in which they all found their place."[19] Gierke believed, however, that he could discern deist and rationalist elements in Althusius's system that arose from his supposed sequestering of religious belief from political theory.[20]

The renewal of interest in Althusius was given further impetus by the work of Carl Joachim Friedrich,[21] who, as Carney states, "in 1932 not only republished the largest part of the 1614 edition of the *Politica* in its original language, but also provided for it an introduction that considerably advanced our knowledge of Althusius's life as well as his thought."[22] Friedrich, contrary to Gierke, focused attention on the concept of the symbiotic association as the foundation of Althusius's political theory and on his religious beliefs as the interpretive key to understanding the concept of symbiosis. Nonetheless, like Gierke, Friedrich conceded that Althusius seemed to be drifting toward deism though, in his judgment, the move was attributable to "the rigid determinism of the dogma of predestination" as it came to expres-

19. Gierke, *Natural Law and the Theory of Society*, 70.

20. According to Gierke, "Althusius ... deduces his system in a rational way from a purely secular concept of society; for him biblical texts are merely examples, and the events of sacred as well as profane history serve as illustrations of the results which have first been reached by rational inference." See Gierke, *The Development of Political Theory*, 70, and cf. 75. Unfortunately, Brian Tierney continues to read Althusius in the same vein as Gierke; see Tierney's *Religion, Law, and the Growth of Constitutional Thought, 1150–1650* (Cambridge: Cambridge University Press, 1982), 71–79.

21. Friedrich was a professor of government at Harvard for many years during which he devoted a considerable portion of his scholarly attention to the work of Althusius. Friedrich's chief works were "Althusius, Johannes," in *Encyclopaedia of the Social Sciences* (New York: Macmillan, 1937), 2:13–14; "Introduction," in *Politica Methodice Digesta of Johannes Althusius*, xv–cxviii; *Johannes Althusius und sein Werk im Rahmen der Entwicklung der Theorie von der Politik* (Berlin: Duncker and Humblot, 1975); and "Preface," in *The Politics of Johannes Althusius*, trans. Frederick S. Carney (London: Eyre and Spottiswoode, 1965), vii–xii.

22. Carney, "Translator's Introduction," ix.

sion in his new science of politics.[23] Friedrich self-consciously read Althusius through the interpretive lens provided by Max Weber, and so concluded that Althusius's alleged biological naturalism (sym*bio*sis) and determinism were rooted in his Calvinist concept of God,[24] that stressing the emotional bonds among persons living in groups led to his formulation of a theory of the corporate state (akin to the collectivist states of Italy and Russia in the 1930s),[25] and that utilitarianism had come to maturity in his version of secularized Calvinism.[26] Despite the evident differences in their appraisals of Althusius, Friedrich shared with Gierke a very high estimate of Althusius's importance, so much so, in fact, that Friedrich considered him to be "the most profound political thinker between Bodin and Hobbes."[27]

In addition to Gierke and Friedrich—the two scholars most responsible for reestablishing Althusius's reputation after a three-hundred-year hiatus—there is a broad array of twentieth-century scholars from various disciplinary backgrounds who have devoted considerable attention to his thought. As might be expected, political theorists and historians have been in the vanguard of scholars assessing the importance of Althusius's contribution to the development of the Western political tradi-

23. Thus, writes Friedrich, "I believe that in order to comprehend adequately the place of Althusius in the history of thought, one must realize that he, like Hobbes, is attempting to develop the implications for a science of politics of the rigid determinism that the dogma of predestination meant in the natural order. How near he came to the elimination of a personal God is shown by the strange and oft repeated sentence: '*Quod Deus est in mundo, lex est in societate*.' God is here already an impersonal, normative force." See Friedrich, "Introduction," lxviii.

24. Friedrich, "Introduction," lxxiii.

25. Friedrich, "Introduction," lxxxviii, lxxxiv–xciv.

26. Friedrich, "Introduction," lxxviii–lxxix.

27. Friedrich, "Introduction," xv.

tion. The older generation of political historians, such as A. J.[28] and R. W. Carlyle,[29] William Archibald Dunning,[30] and John Neville Figgis,[31] all acknowledge a debt of gratitude to Gierke for reviving interest in Althusius, on the one hand, and largely follow his lead in viewing Althusius as an early proponent of social contract as the foundation of an ordered and authoritative political society, on the other.[32] A. P. d'Entrèves,[33] in particular, subscribes to Friedrich's version of the Weber thesis—that Althusius's political theory was an attempt to develop the implications of a deterministic doctrine of predestination for the natural

28. A. J. Carlyle, *Political Liberty: A History of the Conception in the Middle Ages and Modern Times* (Oxford: Oxford University Press, 1941; London: Frank Cass, 1963), 51–57.

29. A. J. and R. W. Carlyle, *A History of Mediaeval Political Theory in the West* (Edinburgh and London: William Blackwood and Sons, 1936), 6:357–63, 371–72, 394–95, 405–13, 498–501.

30. William Archibald Dunning, *A History of Political Theories from Luther to Montesquieu* (New York: Macmillan, 1916), 61–67.

31. John Neville Figgis, *Studies of Political Thought: From Gerson to Grotius, 1414–1625* (Cambridge: Cambridge University Press, 1907), 175–85. Cf. John Neville Figgis, *The Divine Right of Kings*, 2nd ed. (Cambridge: Cambridge University Press, 1922), 106–36, 219–55.

32. Contemporary political historian Quentin Skinner also reiterates Gierke's estimate of Althusius as "the pivotal figure in the evolution of modern constitutionalism" and "as the first political philosopher who shook off 'the whole theocratic conception of the State.'" However, like Gierke's failure to account for Althusius's use of Ramist logic in organizing the subject matter of the *Politica*, Skinner mistakenly concludes: "Althusius [had] the ambition to emancipate the study of 'politics' from the confines of theology and jurisprudence ..." and, thus, "... outlined the principles of a new, secularised political science in his treatise entitled *Politics Methodically Set Forth*." See Quentin Skinner, *The Foundations of Modern Political Thought* (Cambridge: Cambridge University Press, 1978), 2:341–50 (quotes on pp. 341n1, 342, and 350).

33. Alessandro Passerin d'Entrèves, "Giovanni Althusio e il problema metodologico nella storia della filosofia politica e giuridica," *Rivista internazionale di filosofia del dritto* 14 (1934): 109–23.

order—and, on that basis, concludes that Calvinist nominalism led inexorably to Hobbesian voluntarism.[34]

By mid-century, scholars were already skeptical of Gierke's and Friedrich's assessments of the relationship of Althusius's religious beliefs to his political theory and sought to address a broader range of topics in Althusian scholarship. Pierre Mesnard[35] and Frederick Carney,[36] for example, provided extensive analyses of Althusius's constitutionalism, focusing on the institutional foundation of his political theory in the associations of civil society. Stanley Parry addressed the issue of the relationship of political norms to processes in Althusius. He suggested that Althusius's concern with symbiosis is actually a search to find a means for obtaining participation by the people in decisions that rulers conceive to be the demands of natural law.[37]

34. D'Entrèves, "Giovanni Althusio," 115–16. For a response to this allegation and for a fuller treatment of the problem of so-called "Protestant voluntarism," see Grabill, *Rediscovering the Natural Law in Reformed Theological Ethics*, 54–69.

35. Pierre Mesnard, *L'essor de la philosophie politique de XVIe siècle* (Paris: J. Vrin, 1951).

36. Frederick S. Carney, "Associational Thought in Early Calvinism," in *Voluntary Associations: A Study of Groups in Free Societies*, ed. D. B. Robertson (Richmond: John Knox, 1966), 39–53; and Carney, "The Associational Theory of Johannes Althusius: A Study in Calvinist Constitutionalism" (Ph.D. diss., University of Chicago, 1960).

37. Stanley Parry, "The Political Science of Johannes Althusius" (Ph.D. diss., Yale University, 1953), 60–80, 189–201.

In the 1950s and 1960s, Ernst Reibstein,[38] Peter Joachen Winters,[39] Erik Wolf,[40] and Eckhard Feuerherdt[41] focused scholarly attention on the antecedents, application, and role of the natural-law tradition in Althusius's thought. Reibstein and Winters, in particular, disagreed over the extent to which Althusius worked within the natural-law tradition and the way he related it to the moral precepts of the Decalogue. Reibstein argued that Althusius first became acquainted with the natural-law tradition of the Spanish school of Salamanca through Diego Covarruvias's and Fernando Vásquez's writings on Roman law jurisprudence. He contends that Althusius's early conflict with the Herborn theological faculty already evidences his inclination toward a "natural-law interpretation of the Bible"[42] by reducing the commands of the Decalogue to the precepts of natural law. Therefore, when Althusius appeals to profane examples in the *Politica* to illustrate his theory, Reibstein thinks he intentionally employs the humanistic natural-law methodology of the Spanish school with only minor modifications.

Winters responds to Reibstein with a Barthian-style argument claiming precisely the opposite. According to him, Althusius developed a "biblical or Christological interpretation of natural

---

38. Ernst Reibstein, *Johannes Althusius als Fortsetzer der Schule von Salamanca: Untersuchungen zur Ideengeschichte des Recht-Staates und zur altprotestantischen Naturrechtslehr* (Karlsruhe: C. F. Müller, 1955).

39. Peter Joachen Winters, *Die "Politica" des Johannes Althusius und ihre zeitgenössischen Quellen: Zur Grundlegung der politischen Wissenschaft im 16. und im beginnenden 17. Jahrhundert* (Freiburg: Rombach, 1963).

40. Erik Wolf, *Das Problem der Naturrechtslehre: Versuch einer Orienterierung* (Karlsruhe: C. F. Müller, 1964), and Wolf, *Grosse Rechtsdenker der deutschen Geistesgeschichte*, 4th ed. (Tübingen: Mohr, 1963).

41. Eckhard Feuerherdt, *Gesellschaftsvertrag und Naturrecht in der Staatslehre des Johannes Althusius* (Köln: R. Pulm, 1962).

42. Reibstein, *Johannes Althusius als Fortsetzer der Schule von Salamanca*, 13. For more on this altercation, see Friedrich, "Introduction," xxvii–xxix.

law"[43] because, for Althusius, it was not possible to speak either of the Decalogue or the *lex naturalis* except through Christ, the One who is the very fulfillment of the moral law. For this reason, then, Winters insists that Althusius does not appeal to an abstract ontology to ground his formulation of natural law but rather to God's sovereign will and the revelation of his justice ascertained through Scripture alone. Unfortunately, neither Reibstein nor Winters look to antecedents in the Reformed tradition (other than Calvin) to assist in tracing the development of Althusius's doctrine of natural law. More recently, however, several German scholars associated with the Johannes Althusius Gesellschaft have labored to fill in the historical gaps of our knowledge concerning the theological texts, traditions, and institutions that influenced Althusius's thought.[44]

43. Winters, *Die "Politica" des Johannes Althusius und ihre zeitgenössischen Quellen*, 150–51.

44. As a recent addendum to the Reibstein-Winters exchange, Heinrich Janssen has investigated the way in which the Bible functioned as the foundation of Althusius's political theory, particularly with respect to his understanding of law and the relationship between church and state. Beyond stating that Althusius did not develop "a detailed and elaborate 'natural theology,'" Janssen argues parallel to Reibstein that Althusius's doctrine of natural law follows in the scholastic line of Aquinas, Covarruvias, and Vásquez and not in the early Enlightenment line of Grotius and Pufendorf. Heinrich Janssen, *Die Bibel als Grundlage der politischen Theorie des Johannes Althusius* (Frankfurt am Main: Peter Lang, 1992), 95–99 (quote on p. 97). See also the work of Helmut Hollenstein, "Schule und Erziehung bei Althusius, Calvin und Comenius in ihrer Bedeutung für die Gemeinschaftsbildung," in *Jurisprudenz, Politische Theorie und Politische Theologie: Beiträge des Herborner Symposions zum 400. Jahrenstag der Politica des Johannes Althusius 1603–2003*, ed. Frederick S. Carney, Heinz Schilling, and Dieter Wyduckel (Berlin: Duncker and Humblot, 2003), 7–22; Heinz Schilling, "Johannes Althusius und die Konfessionalisierung der Aussenpolitik—oder: Warum gibt es in der Politica keine Theorie der internationalen Beziehungen?," in *Jurisprudenz, Politische Theorie und Politische Theologie*, 47–69; Christoph Strohm, "Althusius' Rechtslehre im Kontext des reformierten Protestantismus," in *Jurisprudenz, Politische Theorie und*

In the early 1970s, scholars began making a concerted effort to probe the theological (covenantal) and political (federalist) dimensions of Althusius's thought. Building on the work of P. S. Gerbrandy,[45] neo-Calvinist James Skillen[46] sought "to discover the place of Althusius in the development of Dutch Calvinist political thought" and, in so doing, challenged Gierke's and Friedrich's understanding of Althusius's religious beliefs and discerned the importance of the concept of symbiotic communities for later Dutch Calvinist political thinkers. Skillen comments that neither Groen van Prinsterer nor Abraham Kuyper display "any direct knowledge of Althusius' writings, yet the most important twentieth-century political thinker from those circles, Herman Dooyeweerd, recognizes in Althusius the kernel of truth that lies at the heart of his own covenantal political perspective."[47] Dooyeweerd praises Althusius for being the first to take account of "internal structural principles in his theory of human symbiosis" but thinks this insight put him "in opposition to the entire medieval-Aristotelian tradition."[48] Unfortunately, Skillen accepts Dooyeweerd's judgment that Althusius developed his

Politische Theologie, 71–102; and Merio Scattola, "Johannes Althusius und das Naturrecht des 16. Jahrhunderts," in *Jurisprudenz, Politische Theorie und Politische Theologie*, 371–96.

45. P. S. Gerbrandy, *National and International Stability: Althusius, Grotius, Van Vollenhoven* (Cambridge, MA: Harvard University Press, 1944).

46. James W. Skillen, "The Development of Calvinistic Political Theory in the Netherlands, with Special Reference to the Thought of Herman Dooyeweerd" (Ph.D. diss., Duke University, 1974), 191–217; Skillen, "The Political Theory of Johannes Althusius," *Philosophia Reformata* 39 (1974): 170–90; and more recently, Skillen, "From Covenant of Grace to Equitable Public Pluralism: The Dutch Calvinist Contribution," *Calvin Theological Journal* 31, no. 1 (1996): 72–77.

47. Skillen, "From Covenant of Grace to Equitable Public Pluralism," 72.

48. Herman Dooyeweerd, *A New Critique of Theoretical Thought*, trans. David H. Freeman and H. de Jongste (Jordan Station, Ont.: Paideia, 1984), 3:662, 662–63; also see Dooyeweerd, *De Strijd om het Souvereiniteitsbegrip in de Moderne Rechts- en Staatsleer* (Amsterdam: H. J. Paris, 1950), 7–8.

doctrine of symbiosis and understanding of common law (i.e., natural law) and proper law (i.e., positive or customary law) along non-Aristotelian, nonscholastic lines.

Skillen is concerned to rebut Friedrich's claim that Althusius, as an Aristotelian, is merely using the concept of symbiosis to develop the Graeco-Roman tradition of state absolutism.[49] However, instead of acknowledging Althusius's obvious debt to Aristotle and the ways in which Althusius's thought is either continuous or discontinuous with Aristotle's, Skillen juxtaposes Dooyeweerd's antiecclesial, antischolastic mentality to Friedrich's position as mutually exclusive alternatives:

> If Friedrich is correct, then there is no conception in Althusius of an internal difference of nature, or independence, of the various human associations. If Dooyeweerd is correct, then we will discover in Althusius a definite limit to the state according to its peculiar nature—a limit which is determined, at least in part, by the peculiar natures (and laws) of other human association which will not permit the state to "devour" the entire community.[50]

Thus, Skillen feels compelled to assent to Dooyeweerd's viewpoint that Althusius had not yet fully separated himself from "the old Roman Catholic culture with its scholastic thinking" to discover "God's order for the creation (including human social life) not the order which the church had sought to impose upon it."[51]

---

49. Friedrich, "Introduction," lii–liii.

50. Skillen, "The Development of Calvinistic Political Theory in the Netherlands," 198–201 (quote on p. 201); and Skillen, "The Political Theory of Johannes Althusius," 177–79.

51. Skillen, "The Political Theory of Johannes Althusius," 172. For criticism of Dooyeweerd's understanding of the nature-grace motif in Thomas Aquinas, which undergirds his antipathy toward scholasticism in general, see Arvin Vos, *Aquinas, Calvin, and Contemporary Protestant Thought: A Critique of Protestant Views on the Thought of Thomas Aquinas* (Washington, DC: Christian University Press, 1985), 128–33, 148–52.

As a result of accepting Dooyeweerd's analysis, Skillen does not appreciate fully the extent to which Althusius utilized the work of such Protestant scholastic writers as Philipp Melanchthon, Heinrich Bullinger (1504–1575), John Calvin (1509–1564), Peter Martyr Vermigli (1499–1562), Jerome Zanchi (1516–1590), Franciscus Junius (1545–1602), and Samuel Rutherford (ca. 1600–1661),[52] on the one hand, and the precise relationships Althusius establishes between the concepts of *jus commune, jus naturale, lex moralis, lex naturalis, lex communis, lex propria,* and *lex divina,* on the other.[53]

---

52. See Robert M. Kingdon, "Althusius' Use of Calvinist Sources in His *Politica*," *Rechtstheorie* 16 (1997): 19–28; Andries Raath and Shaun de Freitas, "Theologico-Political Federalism: The Office of Magistracy and the Legacy of Heinrich Bullinger (1504–1575)," *Westminster Theological Journal* 63 (2001): 285–304; Robert V. Friedeburg, "From Collective Representation to the Right to Individual Defence: James Steuart's *Ius Populi Vindicatum* and the Use of Johannes Althusius' *Politica* in Restoration Scotland," *History of European Ideas* 24, no. 1 (1998): 19–42; John Lewis Marshall, "Natural Law and the Covenant: The Place of Natural Law in the Covenantal Framework of Samuel Rutherford's *Lex, Rex*" (Ph.D. diss., Westminster Theological Seminary, 1995); and Grabill, *Rediscovering the Natural Law in Reformed Theological Ethics.*

53. Neo-Calvinist Gordon Spykman, likewise following Dooyeweerd, falls prey to exactly the same appraisal of Althusius as Skillen does. Like Skillen, Spykman credits Althusius with providing "the systematic climax of Calvinist social thought coming up out of the sixteenth-century Reformation, and with formulating the first clear statement of that complementary principle which in later Calvinist tradition came to be known as sphere sovereignty and sphere universality." However, he contends that it is possible to criticize Althusian social philosophy on a number of dubious points. First, "It betrays remnants of an earlier scholastic notion of a certain hierarchy among social institutions." Second, "It seems that legal norms are derived in part from natural-law theories." Third, "A notion of popular sovereignty is present which leans toward a social contract theory of political authority." Yet, despite these so-called defects, Spykman thinks that Althusius's contribution to a pluralist social philosophy is considerable. Gordon Spykman, "Pluralism: Our Last Best Hope?" *Christian Scholar's Review* 10, no. 2 (1981): 99–115 (quotes on pp. 105 and 107). See also

Contemporary theologians and political theorists, such as J. Wayne Baker, Alain de Benoist, Daniel Elazar, Ken Endo, Thomas Hueglin, Fabrizio Lomonaco, Charles McCoy, and Patrick Riley, who are each interested in reinvigorating federalist political structures, have devoted extensive scholarly attention to Althusius's role as a codifier and theorist of European confederal political arrangements of the late sixteenth and early seventeenth centuries. While each of these scholars would add important qualifications to the following statement by Elazar, they would all agree: "The federal theology that [Reformed Protestantism] articulated ... stimulated the renewed political application of the covenant idea, which was given expression first by political theologians and then by political philosophers such as Althusius and in the next century was secularized by Hobbes, Locke, and Spinoza."[54] Each of the aforementioned scholars has approached

Spykman's *Reformational Theology: A New Paradigm for Doing Dogmatics* (Grand Rapids: Eerdmans, 1992), 20–25. In contrast to Skillen and Spykman, neo-Calvinist social philosopher Henk Woldring presents a more accurate appraisal of the broad parameters of Althusius's social philosophy, specifically with respect to his doctrine of natural law. Unlike Skillen and Spykman, Woldring does not filter Althusius's understanding of natural law through Dooyeweerd's antischolastic interpretive lens. While Woldring fails to place Althusius's doctrine of natural law in the context of his Reformed contemporaries, he does exhibit a rudimentary understanding of the way in which Althusius conceived "natural law as universal principles of law, such as justice, humanity, reasonableness, and fairness, created by God in human nature, which can be clarified by the moral law of the Ten Commandments and by brotherly love." Henk E. S. Woldring, "Multiform Responsibility and the Revitalization of Civil Society," in *Religion, Pluralism, and Public Life: Abraham Kuyper's Legacy for the Twenty-First Century*, ed. Luis E. Lugo (Grand Rapids: Eerdmans, 2000), 178; and Woldring, "The Constitutional State in the Political Philosophy of Johannes Althusius," *European Journal of Law and Economics* 5 (1998): 127–28.

54. Daniel J. Elazar, *The Covenant Tradition in Politics*, vol. 1, *Covenant and Polity in Biblical Israel: Biblical Foundations and Jewish Expressions* (New Brunswick, NJ: Transaction, 1995), 26.

the matter of Althusius's contribution to the development of federalism from different but complementary perspectives.[55]

J. Wayne Baker,[56] Fabrizio Lomonaco,[57] and Charles McCoy,[58] for example, focus on the relationship of Reformed covenantal theology to federal theories of government in the post-Reformation

55. Incidentally, Eric Voegelin stands alone among twentieth-century political philosophers and intellectual historians with his unilaterally negative assessment of Althusius for his use of the Ramist method: "The use of the Ramist method will aid us in fixing the rank of Althusius' work—which is still overrated as a consequence of Otto von Gierke's monograph. The *Politica* is by far the most solid work of the Calvinist monarchomachic group; ... it is the work of an experienced practical lawyer who could digest his rich knowledge, with the aid of his 'method,' into a well-ordered book; but it is definitely not the work of a great political thinker." One suspects, however, that Voegelin's criticism relates more to his displeasure with Althusius's successful integration of Reformed ecclesiology with juridical structure than it does to Althusius's clear repudiation of Jean Bodin's integration of Roman Catholic ecclesiology (*plenitudo potestatis*) to the issue of sovereignty in the commonwealth. Voegelin's criticism of Althusius also seems to summarize and restate Gierke's earlier criticism (cf. Gierke, *The Development of Political Theory*, 22–23). See Eric Voegelin, *The Collected Works of Eric Voegelin*, vol. 23, *History of Political Ideas*, vol. 5, *Religion and the Rise of Modernity*, ed. James L. Wiser (Columbia: University of Missouri Press, 1998), 55–59 (quote on p. 56).

56. J. Wayne Baker and Charles S. McCoy, *Fountainhead of Federalism: Heinrich Bullinger and the Covenantal Tradition* (Louisville: Westminster John Knox, 1991), chap. 2, "The Development of the Federal Theological Tradition," 29–44; chap. 3, "Federal Political Philosophy: Mornay and Althusius," 45–62.

57. Fabrizio Lomonaco, "Huguenot Critical Theory and 'Ius Maiestatis' in Huber and Althusius," in *New Essays on the Political Thought of the Huguenots of the Refuge*, ed. John Christian Laursen (Leiden: Brill, 1995), 171–92.

58. Charles McCoy, "The Centrality of Covenant in the Political Philosophy of Johannes Althusius," in *Politische Theorie des Johannes Althusius*, ed. Karl-Wilhelm Dahm, Werner Krawietz, and Dieter Wyduckel (Berlin: Duncker and Humblot, 1988), 187–99; and McCoy, "Der Bund als Grundmetapher in der Politica des Johannes Althusius," in *Gottes Zukunft—Zukunft der Welt* (München: Chr. Kaiser, 1986), 332–44.

era of England, Germany, the Netherlands, Switzerland, and France. They are interested in showing that Althusius's federal political philosophy arose out of the political and theological climate of the time. According to Baker and McCoy, federal political models "were widely practiced, especially in areas influenced by the Reformed tradition coming from Zurich and Bullinger. Althusius could draw, therefore, on many actual examples of operating federal polities as well as scholarly treatises of the past and present on government."[59] Furthermore, McCoy insists that covenant is the root metaphor by means of which Althusius understands human society. In fact, he thinks the concept of covenant (*pactum*) is what ties together the various streams of Greek, Roman, biblical, and sixteenth-century polities from which Althusius draws.[60]

During his lifetime, Jewish scholar Daniel Elazar was at the forefront of the twentieth-century interdisciplinary and ecumenical interest in assessing Althusius's contribution to the development of federalism. Throughout publications spanning more than three decades, Elazar argued that the arduous road to modern democracy began with the Protestant Reformation's revival of the biblical-covenantal tradition of politics.[61] In his

59. Baker and McCoy, *Fountainhead of Federalism*, 50.

60. According to McCoy, "In the hands of Althusius, immersed as he is in the federalism of Herborn, the covenant as fundamental political principle encompasses the contractualism of Roman law and the centrality of politics for human living found in the Aristotelian and natural-law traditions." See McCoy, "The Centrality of Covenant in the Political Philosophy of Johannes Althusius," 190.

61. In this respect, Daniel Elazar's four-volume *Covenant Tradition in Politics* series (New Brunswick, NJ: Transaction, 1995–1998) is his crowning achievement: vol. 1, *Covenant and Polity in Biblical Israel: Biblical Foundations and Jewish Expressions* (1995); vol. 2, *Covenant and Commonwealth: From Christian Separation Through the Protestant Reformation* (1996); vol. 3, *Covenant and Constitutionalism: The Great Frontier and the Matrix of Federal Democracy* (1998); and vol. 4, *Covenant and Civil Society: The Constitutional Matrix of Modern Democracy* (1998).

introductory essay to Carney's translation of the *Politica*, Elazar contended that exponents of Reformed Protestantism developed a theology and politics that set the Western world on the road to popular self-government, emphasizing liberty and equality: "Only at the end of the first century of the Reformation did a political philosopher emerge out of the Reformed tradition to build a systematic political philosophy out of the Reformed experience by synthesizing the political experience of the Holy Roman Empire with the political ideas of the covenant theology of Reformed Protestantism."[62] Elazar's main concern with the *religious* foundation of federalism centers in its origin in the covenantal structure of the Old Testament. Indeed, the argument could be made that Elazar's legacy consists of having shown how the covenantal basis of Judaism was reiterated in Reformed Protestantism and later expressed in the federalist principles of the American polity.[63]

62. Daniel J. Elazar, "Althusius' Grand Design for a Federal Commonwealth," in *Politica,* ed. and trans. Frederick S. Carney, xxxv. A little further down the page, Elazar summarizes Althusius's principal contribution as follows: "Althusius' *Politica* was the first book to present a comprehensive theory of federal republicanism rooted in a covenantal view of human society derived from, but not dependent on, a theological system. It presented a theory of polity-building based on the polity as a compound political association established by its citizens through their primary associations on the basis of consent rather than a reified state imposed by a ruler or an elite." Cf. Elazar, *Covenant and Polity in Biblical Israel*, 26; and Elazar, *Covenant and Civil Society*, 1–2, 20–21, 27–28.

63. Thomas Hueglin, in contrast to Elazar, argues that while the American Federalists drew from the older European tradition of federalism, for example, in Montesquieu's *The Spirit of Laws*—and, through Montesquieu's use of historical examples there, Althusius's theory of consociational federalism—"an argument can be made that the Federalists' interpretation constituted a deliberate and radical break with [the older European] tradition" of federalism. Hueglin, "Federalism at the Crossroads: Old Meanings, New Significance," *Canadian Journal of Political Science* 36, no. 2 (2003): 275–94 (quote on p. 276).

By focusing on the constitutional dimensions of Althusius's federalism, contemporary political theorists and legal scholars such as Michael Behnen,[64] Alain de Benoist,[65] Ken Endo,[66] Thomas Hueglin,[67] Patrick Riley,[68] and Nicholas Aroney[69] have provided nuanced assessments of Althusius's political theory as a form of medieval corporatism and modern constitutionalism, on the one hand, and argued that his doctrine of subsidiarity can be seen as more or less consonant with modern federal (territorial) and confederal (nonterritorial) polities, on the other. Hueglin,

64. Michael Behnen, "Herrscherbild und Herrschaftstechnik in der 'Politica' des Johannes Althusius," *Zeitschrift für historische Forschung* 11 (1984): 417–72.

65. Alain de Benoist, "The First Federalist: Johannes Althusius," *Krisis* 22 (1999): 2–34.

66. Ken Endo, "The Principle of Subsidiarity: From Johannes Althusius to Jacques Delors," *Hokkaido Law Review* 44, no. 6 (1994): 553–652.

67. Thomas Hueglin, "Taking Stock: Althusius After Four Hundred Years," in *Jurisprudenz, Politische Theorie und Politische Theologie*, 305–17; Heuglin, "Federalism at the Crossroads," 275–94; Hueglin, "Covenant and Federalism in the Politics of Althusius," in *The Covenant Connection: From Federal Theology to Modern Federalism*, ed. Daniel J. Elazar and John Kincaid (Lanham: Lexington, 2000), 31–54; Hueglin, *Early Modern Concepts for a Late Modern World*; Hueglin, "Have We Studied the Wrong Authors? On the Relevance of Johannes Althusius," *Studies in Political Thought* 1, no. 1 (1992): 75–93; Hueglin, "Johannes Althusius: Medieval Constitutionalist or Modern Federalist?" *Publius: The Journal of Federalism* 9, no. 4 (1979): 9–41; and Hueglin, *Sozietaler Föderalismus: Die politische Theorie des Johannes Althusius* (Berlin: De Gruyter, 1991).

68. Patrick Riley, "Three Seventeenth Century German Theorists of Federalism: Althusius, Hugo, and Leibniz," *Publius: The Journal of Federalism* 6, no. 3 (1976): 7–41.

69. Nicholas Aroney, "Formation, Representation and Amendment in Federal Constitutions," *The American Journal of Comparative Law* 54 (2006): 277–336; and Aroney, "Althusius at the Antipodes: The *Politica* and Australian Federalism," in *Jurisprudenz, Politische Theorie und Politische Theologie*, 529–46.

in particular, has been a vigorous proponent of the confederal tradition of political thought that Althusius represents. He writes:

> The classical canon of political thought has remained committed to the idea of state power as an independent variable of societal organization. Given the pluralization of power among political, economic, and social actors in the modern polity, the continued adherence to that canon amounts to nothing less than "studying the wrong authors." Althusius reminds us not only that there is an alternative tradition of political thought that emphasizes the horizontal over the vertical in political life. His conceptualization of politics also serves as a reminder that the sovereign territorial state is but an episode in the history of political civilization.[70]

The research team of Jacques Delors, president of the European Commission during the long and difficult gestation period of the Maastricht Treaty in the European Union, thinks the modern beginning of subsidiarity as a guiding principle of power allocation in plural systems of governance is to be found in a 1571 resolution passed by the Synod of Emden to govern the relationship between parishes and general synods. The researchers attribute the genesis of this political principle to Calvinist "federal theology, Emden and Althusius,"[71] which predates Pope

---

70. Hueglin, "Have We Studied the Wrong Authors?," 89.

71. Hueglin, *Early Modern Concepts for a Late Modern World*, 152. Cf. Endo, "The Principle of Subsidiarity," 629–32. Recent publications sponsored by the Johannes Althusius Gesellschaft have investigated such topics as consensus and consociation in early modern federalism and the concept of subsidiarity in church, state, and society. The massive two-volume *Althusius-Bibliographie* appeared in 1973 as the first publication of the recently founded Johannes Althusius Gesellschaft, now associated with the faculty of law at the Technical University of Dresden and renamed as the Society for Research on Early Modern Legal Theory and Constitutional History (http://www.althusius.de), and organizes all that was written by Althusius or about his life and work up to the date of its publication. The major publications of the Society from latest to earliest are as follows: Frederick S.

Pius XI's famous description of the doctrine of subsidiarity in the 1931 encyclical *Quadragesimo Anno* (nos. 79–80) by nearly three and one-half centuries.

The *Dicaeologicae*: Significance and Overview

As Althusius indicates in the preface to the *Dicaeologicae*, he was not satisfied with the synthesis of law set forth in the *Jurisprudentiae Romanae*. Thus, for the next several years he sought to perfect his system in an effort to make it maximally coherent and comprehensive. Already in the year 1591, recounts Gierke, "Althusius gave to Corvinus, his publisher in Herborn who desired a new edition, a brief outline of his revised system which was prefixed to the edition of 1592 and the later Herborn editions under the title of *Epitome et brevis ... Dicaeologicae Romanae*."[72] The expansion of this project into a full account of the whole body of law was not completed until the publication of *Dicaeologicae*

Carney, Heinz Schilling, and Dieter Wyduckel, eds., *Jurisprudenz, politische Theorie und politische Theologie* (2004); Emilio Bonfatti, Giuseppe Duso, and Merio Scattola, eds., *Politisches Begriffe und historisches Umfeld in der Politica methodice digesta des Johannes Althusius* (Wiesbaden: Harrassowitz, 2002); Peter Blickle, Thomas Hüglin, and Dieter Wyduckel, eds., *Subsidiarität als rechtliches und politisches Ordnungsprinzip in Kirche, Staat und Gesellschaft: Genese, Geltungsgrundlagen und Perspektiven an der Schwelle des dritten Jahrtausends* (Berlin: Duncker and Humblot, 2002); Giuseppe Duso, Werner Krawietz, and Dieter Wyduckel, eds., *Konsens und Konsoziation in der Politischen Theorie des frühen Föderalismus* (Berlin: Duncker and Humblot, 1997); Karl-Wilhelm Dahm, Werner Krawietz, and Dieter Wyduckel, eds., *Politische Theorie des Johannes Althusius* (1988); and Dieter Wyduckel, *Althusius-Bibliographie: Bibliographie zur politischen Ideengeschichte und Staatslehre, zum Staatsrecht und zur Verfassungsgeschichte des 16. bis 18. Jahrhunderts*, 2 vols., ed. Hans Ulrich Scupin and Ulrich Scheuner (Berlin: Duncker and Humblot, 1973). For a review of the latter work, see Theo Veen, "Een *Fundgrube* voor de historische wetenschap: de *Althusius-Bibliografie*," *Bijdragen en Mededelingen Betreffende de Geschiedenis der Nederlanden* 94, no. 1 (1979): 89–96.

72. Gierke, *The Development of Political Theory*, 54.

libri tres, totum et universum jus, quo utimur, methodice complectentes in 1617 at Herborn.

Yet, in Gierke's judgment, the material of the *Dicaeologicae* is systematized to the point of being contrived. "From the first principles down to the most minute details it is deduced with inexorable rigor, one might even say fanaticism," he states disparagingly of Althusius's use of Ramist logic. "At every point the successive division of concepts is worked out by the force of dialectic. Often indeed the required dichotomy can only be set up by recourse to somewhat arbitrary antitheses, such as 'general' and 'special.'"[73] While Gierke was critical in general of Ramist logic and scholastic method, Berman has a firmer and more subtle grasp of the philosophical, theological, and philological antecedents of the new legal science of the sixteenth and early seventeenth century. The *Jurisprudentiae Romanae* and the *Dicaeologicae*, which were republished many times in the seventeenth and eighteenth centuries, writes Berman, "were in the tradition of Lagus and Vigelius; like them, Althusius divided all law into public law and private law, subdivided private law into ownership and obligation, subdivided obligation into contract, tort, and unjust enrichment, and sought to deduce from general concepts and general principles the detailed rules applicable to individual transactions."[74] The systematization of law that took place in the sixteenth century in the work of Apel, Lagus, Vigelius, and Althusius "remain to this day the basic 'topics' of Western legal science.[75]

73. Gierke, *The Development of Political Theory*, 54.

74. Berman, *Law and Revolution, II*, 125–26.

75. Berman, *Law and Revolution, II*, 125. Berman's assessment stands in stark contrast to Gierke's, who writes, "And if on the whole this intricate and ingenious system gained no lasting success, it served at least, as its author hoped, to facilitate and clarify the study of law, and in fact several rearrangements first made by him became in course of time generally accepted." See Gierke, *The Development of Political Theory*, 55.

Before concluding, I will provide a brief overview of the *Dicaeologicae*, in which I rely upon Gierke's helpful schematic,[76] and will state in broad strokes the significance of the material that has been translated in the present volume. Althusius divides the science of law into a general and a special part, which are distinguished as the *membra* and the *species* of jurisprudence. As elements (*membra*) of all legal relations, a distinction is drawn between the *negotium symbioticum*, that is, the activity of human life as leading to the establishment of rights, and the *jus*, or law (right). Althusius divides the general part (1.1–34) into two sections.

The first section concerns the *negotium symbioticum* and the *factum civile*, or the business of this world. Its elements are things and persons. Persons are considered only insofar as their qualities, conditions, and strivings involve legal differences; following the strictures of Ramist method Althusius will not attempt to analyze aspects of persons that come into play in other disciplines such as political science, ethics, theology, or history (c. 1, nos. 9–10). Next, he analyzes things, their partition into real and ideal parts and their division into individual and composite things, with further subdivisions (c. 1, nos. 11–44). Then, he treats the person as *homo juris communionem habens*, which is divided into two species: first, individual persons and the influence of inherited and acquired status (c. 5–6) and, second, the natural and voluntary associations of persons (c. 7–8). After this comes a section on the theory of the human act whereby the person constitutes things as elements of social relations (c. 9–12). Last comes a consideration of the various species of *factum civile* (c. 12, nos. 12–17).

The second section treats *jus*, which is divided into the theory of *constitutio juris* (or objective law) and *species juris* (or subjective law). The establishment of law takes place through a rational

76. This overview of the *Dicaeologicae* is a summary of a longer, more detailed treatment by Gierke in *The Development of Political Theory*, 55–59.

deduction from the essential nature of *negotium*. Natural law (or common law as Althusius refers to it), which is a significant source of law in general, is set up by common right reason (*recta ratio communis*) in accordance with the general requirements of human society (c. 13). Positive law (or individual, principal law as Althusius refers to it) is derived from the *recta ratio specialis* according to the special requirements of local patterns or customs of life (c. 14). The latter, to be considered law at all, however, must conform to the first principles of natural law, but, at the same time, to remain positive law, it must differ from natural law in its ability to adapt to new concrete circumstances. In chapters thirteen and fourteen respectively, which appear in the present volume, Althusius treats in some depth first what law is and what normative significance the law inscribed on the heart has for civil law (c. 13) and then discusses the various species of written and unwritten positive law (c. 14).

He next addresses *dominium* and *obligatio*, which, as Gierke states, are in general distinguished as "real right" and "personal right."[77] Under *dominium* he treats various species of ownership and extends his discussion to a possession of things (c. 18–21). However, so-called real rights in the property of others can take various forms of servitude, which he analyzes in detail (c. 22–24); they can also be understood in terms of power relations, which he addresses in considerable depth (c. 25–33). It is important to be clear that Althusius classifies these issues under *dominium* because they partake of the nature of ownership. Under the general rubric of power (*potestas*), he treats various forms of liberty such as the subjective rights of reputation, dignity, chastity, and bodily integrity (c. 25–26). Under the topic of alien power, he analyzes private power (c. 27–31) and public power (c. 32–33). The final two chapters of the translation herein, chapters 32 and 33, concern the general nature of public power in civil and ecclesiastical realms (c. 32) and, significantly, the limitations to

77. Gierke, *The Development of Political Theory*, 56.

public power and civil authority (c. 33). He concludes this section with a general treatment of the second species of subjective right: obligation (c. 34). This concludes Althusius's discussion of the general part of all legal relations.

The special part, or *Species Dicaeologicae*, is divided into the *Dicaeodotica* and the *Dicaeocritica*. The *Dicaeodotica* concerns the distribution of rights among people, and is divided into the *Dicaeodotica acquirens* (acquisition) and *amittens* (obligation). The remaining sections of book 1 concern the topic of how rights are acquired. After stating general principles governing the acquisition of rights (c. 35), Althusius takes up the acquisition of ownership, where he also discusses the right of inheritance (c. 36–63). He next addresses various relationships of obligation through contracts or delicts. Following this, he then proceeds to give a full treatment of the creation and operation of contracts and their several species (c. 64–97). Book 1 ends with a treatment of delicts that is expanded into a complete system of criminal law (c. 98–146).

Book 2 of the *Dicaeologicae* is concerned with the loss of rights. It deals first with the extinction of rights in general (2.1–11), and is then followed by a discussion of the special modes in which ownership and possession can be abrogated (c. 12–13). Next is a treatment of the modes by which obligations can be terminated, particularly with respect to their performance (c. 14–22). Finally, there is a brief discussion of the discharge of obligation with respect to delicts (c. 23).

The *Dicaeocritica* concerns the matter of rights in dispute and of their trial and adjudication. This is the subject of book 3, wherein Althusius provides a systematic treatment of the whole law of procedure, including the law of actions.

Given our debt to Gierke in general for reviving interest in Althusius and mine in particular for his schematic of the *Dicaeologicae*, it seems fitting to allow him a final opportunity to shed light on the significance of the syndic of Emden's whole body of law:

The reception of doctrines of public law in the system of civil law is not itself peculiar to Althusius. As the whole exegetic literature since the Gloss upon the Corpus Iuris Civilis had brought the study of questions of public law within the sphere of the civil law, this arrangement was preserved by the "methodists." Of these but few attempted to sunder public law from private law as a separate domain; on the contrary, this was regularly treated as coming within the bounds of private law and more especially the law of Persons. But as these "publicistic" admixtures had grown out of the external condition of the original texts, they remained all the more an incidental and occasional adjunct. On the other hand, Althusius, who in the *Jurisprudentia Romana* had done much like his predecessors, set to work in full earnest in the *Dicaeologica* [*sic*] to incorporate the whole body of public law into the Civilian system. Here indeed, as he asserted and maintained at all points the theories already developed in his *Politics*, he had no difficulty in distributing the relations of public law under the rubrics of private law. The result was a unified legal structure, erected wholly in the style of private law and yet covering the groundwork of public law, the like of which was hardly ever constructed before or since.[78]

78. Gierke, *The Development of Political Theory*, 57–58.

A Demonstrative Theory of Natural Law: Johannes Althusius and the Rise of Calvinist Jurisprudence

John Witte, Jr.[1]

In the past decade, a small cottage industry of important new books and articles has emerged dedicated to documenting distinctive Calvinist contributions to the development of Western theories of natural law. Rejecting the stern anti-naturalism of Karl Barth and his many followers, several writers have shown that early modern Calvinists throughout Europe and North America used natural law concepts and methods to work out their ideas and institutions of law, politics, ethics, and society. Some of these early Calvinist contributions were continuous with the teachings of the *ius commune*; others bore the distinct theological marks

1. This text is adapted in part from my article, "A Demonstrative Theory of Natural Law: The Original Contribution of Johannes Althusius," in *Public Theology for a Global Society: Essays in Honor of Max L. Stackhouse*, ed. Deirdre King Hainsworth and Scott R. Paeth (Grand Rapids: Eerdmans, 2010), 21–36, and is used herein with permission.

of John Calvin and his diverse followers.[2] Natural law was not, as Barth[3] and his followers taught, a scholastic hangover or Enlightenment intoxicant that clear-eyed Calvinists rejected. It was a vital and variant part of early modern Calvinist teachings.

In this essay, I focus on the natural-law theory of one such early modern Calvinist jurist, Johannes Althusius (1557–1638). Althusius has been called "the clearest and most profound thinker which Calvinism has produced in the realm of political science

---

2. Christoph Strohm, "Recht und Jurisprudenz im reformierten Protestantismus 1550–1650," *Zeitschrift der Savigny-Stiftung für Reschtsgeschichte* (KA) 123 (2006): 453–93; idem, *Ethik im frühen Calvinismus* (Berlin: De Gruyter, 1996); idem, *Calvinismus und Recht* (Tübingen: Mohr Siebeck, 2008); Stephen Grabill, *Rediscovering the Natural Law in Reformed Theological Ethics* (Grand Rapids: Eerdmans, 2005); Frederick S. Carney, Heinz Schilling, and Dieter Wyduckel, eds., *Jurisprudenz, politische Theorie und politische Theologie* (Berlin: Duncker & Humblot, 2004); Volker Heise, *Der calvinistische Einfluss auf das humanistische Rechtsdenken exemplarisch dargestellt an den "Commentarii de iure civili" von Hugo Donellus (1527–1591)* (Göttingen: V&R unipress, 2004); Philip S. Gorski, *The Disciplinary Revolution: Calvinism and the Rise of the State in Early Modern Europe* (Chicago: University of Chicago Press, 2003); John W. Sap, *Paving the Way for Revolution: Calvinism and the Struggle for a Democratic Constitutional State* (Amsterdam: VU Uitgeverij, 2001); David W. Hall, *The Genevan Reformation and the American Founding* (Lanham: Lexington, 2003); David T. Ball, *The Historical Origins of Judicial Review, 1536–1803: The Duty to Resist Tyranny* (Lewiston: Edwin Mellen, 2005); Rufus Black, *Christian Moral Realism: Natural Law, Narrative, Virtue, and the Gospel* (Oxford: Oxford University Press, 2000); Dale Van Kley, *The Religious Origins of the French Revolution: From Calvin to the Civil Constitution, 1560–1791* (New Haven: Yale University Press, 1996). See further sources and discussion in my book *The Reformation of Rights: Law, Religion, and Human Rights in Early Modern Calvinism* (Cambridge: Cambridge University Press, 2007).

3. See George Hunsinger, "Karl Barth," in *The Teachings of Modern Christianity on Law, Politics, and Human Nature*, ed. John Witte, Jr. and Frank S. Alexander, 2 vols. (New York: Columbia University Press, 2005), 1:352–80, 2:280–306, and Grabill, *Rediscovering the Natural Law*, 21–53.

and jurisprudence."[4] Born in a tiny German town in Wittgenstein-Berleburg in 1557, he studied law, theology, philosophy, and the classics at the universities of Cologne, Geneva, Heidelberg, and Basel, working intermittently with such Calvinist worthies as François Hotman and Denis Godefroy. He took his doctorate in canon law and civil law (*doctor juris utriusque*) from the University of Basel. His first appointment came in 1586 as lecturer in Roman law and philosophy at the Herborn Academy, a new Calvinist college that was attracting faculty and students from throughout Europe. Among his new Herborn colleagues was Caspar Olevianus, coauthor of the Heidelberg Catechism (1563), a Calvinist creedal landmark. In 1594, Althusius was promoted to Professor of Law at Herborn, and served twice as rector of the Academy in 1597 and 1602. His later years there, however, were marked by repeated internal controversy. Particularly notable

4. Carl J. Friedrich, "Introductory Remarks," to Johannes Althusius, *Politica methodice digesta atque exemplis sacris & profanis illustrata*, 3rd ed. (Herborn, 1614), reprinted as *Politica methodice digesta of Johannes Althusius (Althaus)*, ed. Carl J. Friedrich (Cambridge, MA: Harvard University Press, 1932), xviii. For Althusius's writings and reputation, see *Althusius-Bibliographie. Bibliographie zur politischen Ideengeschichte und Staatslehre, zum Staatsrecht und zur Verfassungsgeschichte des 16. bis 18. Jahrhunderts*, ed. Hans Ulrich Scupin et al. (Berlin: Duncker & Humblot, 1973), updated in Dieter Wyduckel, "Einleitung, Literaturverzeichnis," in Johannes Althusius, *Politik*, trans. Heinrich Janssen, ed. Dieter Wyduckel (Berlin: Duncker & Humblot, 2003), vii–lxxxii. Among numerous studies, see Friedrich, "Introductory Remarks," xv–xcix; Thomas O. Hueglin, *Early Modern Concepts for a Late Modern World: Althusius on Community and Federalism* (Waterloo, Ont.: Wilfrid Laurier University Press, 1999); Otto von Gierke, *The Development of Political Theory*, trans. Bernard Freyd (New York: H. Fertig, 1966); Karl-Wilhelm Dahm, Werner Krawietz, and Dieter Wyduckel, eds., *Politische Theorie des Johannes Althusius* (Berlin: Duncker & Humblot, 1988); Heinz Antholz, *Die politische Wirksamkeit des Johannes Althusius in Emden* (Aurich: Abhandlungen und Vorträge zur Ostfriesische Landschaft, 1955); Erik Wolf, *Grosse Rechtsdenker der deutschen Geistesgeschichte*, 4th ed. (Tübingen: Mohr, 1963), 177–219.

was Althusius's debate with his colleagues about the modern uses of biblical law.

In 1604, Althusius moved to Emden, an important seaport city in eastern Frisia, near the border of the Holy Roman Empire and the newly united Netherlands. Emden was a major center for Calvinist refugees from throughout Europe, and an emerging intellectual and missionary center for the spread of Calvinism. Althusius was appointed as legal counsel for the city (*Stadtsyndicus*) and became deeply involved in the city's multiple legal, commercial, and diplomatic negotiations. He played a leading role in helping Emden wrest greater independence from the local territorial count and nobles, an accomplishment that made him something of a local hero. Though he continued to give lectures, he did not hold a formal university position thereafter and turned down attractive professorships in Leiden and Franeker. Althusius was also elected as an elder of the Reformed church of Emden in 1617, and served for years on the Emden Consistory, hearing cases on spiritual, moral, and family questions much like John Calvin had done a half century before on the Genevan Consistory.

While these local achievements in church and state were notable in their day, Althusius's more enduring contributions came through his writings. Though he left a score of books, it was especially his trilogy of works on ethics, politics, and law that made signature contributions. His two-volume *Civil Interactions* of 1601 (expanded in 1611), worked out a system of "ethical habits and techniques" of "speaking and listening," "proclamation and silence," to guide rhetoric, dialogue, and persuasion in various social institutions, most notably in the church and the state.[5] His massive *Politics* of 1603 (revised in 1610 and again in 1614), set forth a comprehensive theory of social, political, and legal order and activity, and the forms and norms of sovereignty, authority,

5. Johannes Althusius, *Civilis conversationis libri duo recogniti et aucti. Methodice digesti et exemplis sacris et profanis passim illustrati* (Hannover, 1601, 1611).

and liberty that obtain within each sphere.[6] His three-volume *Theory of Justice* (1617) laid the groundwork for a comprehensive theory of law and justice, with attention to the rights and liberties of private persons and the various private and public associations that they formed.[7]

Althusius presented these three big tracts as "comprehensive," "total," and "universal" accounts of the disciplines of ethics, politics, and law respectively. Each tract was amply illustrated by "sacred and profane examples." Each tract used the dialectical method of the French Calvinist logician Peter Ramus, by which Althusius defined the first principles of these three disciplines, and then divided their constituent precepts and practices into a series of ever more particular binary opposites. Each tract drew on hundreds of scholarly sources—sundry ancient Greeks and Romans, the Bible and Apocrypha, various apostolic and patristic writers, numerous medieval theologians, philosophers, and civilians, a few canonists and rabbis, various Protestant jurists, numerous contemporary Catholic and Protestant political writers, and several collections of civil, imperial, feudal, and urban law, ancient and modern. Using this vast library, Althusius's ambition was to explore deeply the foundations and fundamentals of law, politics, and society, and to bring the insights of the entire Western tradition into a "total" and "universal" theory that

6. Johannes Althusius, *Politica methodice digesta atque exemplis sacris & profanis illustrata*, 3rd ed. (Herborn, 1614), reprinted as *Politica methodice digesta*, ed. Carl J. Friedrich. See abridged English translation, *Politica*, ed. and trans. F. S. Carney (Indianapolis: Liberty Fund, 1995); abridged German text of the 1614 edition in Althusius, *Politik*, ed. Dieter Wyduckel; and the Latin and English version of the preface to the 1610 edition in John Christian Laursen, ed., *New Essays on the Political Thought of the Huguenots of the Refuge* (Leiden: Brill, 1995), 193–201. I have used the 1614 Friedrich edition unless otherwise noted, and adapted the English translation by F. S. Carney in *Politica* (hereafter cited as *Pol.*).

7. Johannes Althusius, *Dicaeologicae libri tres, totum et universum Jus, quo utimur, methodice complectentes* (Herborn, 1617; Frankfurt, 1618); I have used the 1618 edition throughout (hereafter cited as *Dic.*).

would appeal not only to fellow Calvinists and countrymen but to anyone in his world of Christendom who was serious about faith and order, authority and liberty.

Natural Law, Common Law, and Positive Law

Natural law was one of the foundations of Althusius's impressive new system. (Complex theories of natural rights, human nature, social contract, divine covenant, symbiotic association, written constitutionalism, and political federalism were amongst the other foundations.) Particularly in later editions of his *Politics* and in his *Theory of Justice*, Althusius set out a "demonstrative theory" of natural law—a theory designed to "demonstrate" the ultimate concordance between biblical and rational, Christian and classical teachings on the nature and purpose of law.[8]

Althusius effectively merged the hierarchies of law developed by fellow jurists and theologians of his day, both Catholic and Protestant. Civil law and canon law jurists generally distinguished three main types of law: (1) the natural law or law of nature (*ius naturale, lex naturae*), the set of immutable principles of reason and conscience that are supreme in authority and divinity; (2) the law of nations or common law (*ius gentium, ius commune, lex communis*), the legal principles and procedures that are common to multiple political communities and often the basis for

8. I take this phrase from the Danish Protestant jurist and theologian, Nicolaus Hemming, whose work straddled the Lutheran and Calvinist worlds of law. Writing in the later sixteenth century, Hemming developed what he called a "demonstrative method of natural law," which aimed to demonstrate the natural universality and superiority of the Decalogue as a source and summary of natural law. He adduced hundreds of ancient Greek and Roman passages that he saw to be consistent with conventional Protestant interpretations of the Ten Commandments and its biblical echoes. See Nicolaus Hemming, *De lege naturae apodicta methodus* (Wittenberg, 1563), and further analysis in my book *Law and Protestantism: The Legal Teachings of the Lutheran Reformation* (Cambridge: Cambridge University Press, 2002), 139.

treaties and other diplomatic conventions; and (3) the civil law or positive law (*ius civile, ius positivum*), the statutes, customs, and cases of various states, churches, fiefdoms, manors, and other local political communities.[9] Theologians and moralists, in turn, generally distinguished three main types of biblical law: (1) moral law (*lex moralis*), the enduring moral teachings of the Decalogue and the New Testament; (2) juridical or forensic law (*lex juridicales, ius forensi*), the rules and procedures by which ancient Israelites and apostolic Christians governed their religious and civil communities; and (3) ceremonial law (*lex ceremonialis*), the Mosaic laws of personal diet, ritual sacrifice, priestly life, and the like that governed the religious life of the ancient Israelites. Some theologians saw parallels between these three ancient types of biblical law and the three layers of modern Catholic and Protestant church law that governed, respectively, the essentials of doctrine and morality, the commonplaces of ecclesiastical polity and property, and the discretionary aspects (the adiaphora) of local church life.[10]

In his early writings, Althusius repeated these traditional hierarchies of law. In his later writings, however, most fully in his 1617 *Theory of Justice*, he collapsed these traditional legal terms and hierarchies into two main types of law: natural laws and positive laws. Furthermore, he subsumed most of the other traditional types of law within these two categories. He treated the moral laws of the Bible and the common laws of nations as two visible forms of the same invisible natural law hidden within each person's reason and conscience. He regarded the laws of ancient Israelites and of modern churches as two types of positive law that stood alongside the positive laws of historical and modern states. The modern validity of all these positive laws turned on their concordance with natural law. Their modern utility for the state turned on their compliance with the fundamental law

9. *Dic.* 1.13.6, 10.

10. *Pol.* 21.35–40; *Pol.* 22.1–12; *Pol.* Preface (1603, 1610, and 1614 eds.).

(*lex fundamentalis*) of the community, which ideally would be articulated by a written constitution.[11]

Natural law is "the will of God for men," Althusius argued. God has "written this natural law" on the hearts, souls, minds, and consciences of all persons, as Romans 2:15 and sundry other biblical and classical sources make clear. Everyone, by his or her very nature, thus has the "ideas (*notitiae*) and inclinations (*inclinationes*) of this natural law" born within them. Some of these "natural inclinations" are common to humans and animals. Like animals, humans by nature are inclined to "preserve their lives and to procure the necessities to remain alive." They are inclined to defend themselves against force and *force majeure*. They are inclined to ally themselves with others and to rally around natural leaders to aid them in their self-defense. They are inclined to "procreate by the union of male and female and to educate their natural-born children." They are inclined to care for themselves and for their loved ones when they are sick, hurt, or ailing. Self-preservation, self-protection, and self-perpetuation are "natural inclinations" that the natural law teaches to persons and animals alike.[12]

The natural law also teaches persons higher ideas that appeal uniquely to human reason and conscience. By them, "a man understands what justice is, and is impelled by this hidden natural instinct to do what is just and to avoid what is unjust." Through the natural law, God commands all persons to "live a life that is at once pious and holy, just and proper." He teaches them the natural "duties of love that are to be performed toward God and one's neighbor." He sets out the basic "rules of living, obeying, and administering" that must govern all persons and associations. He sets forth "general principles of goodness and

11. *Pol.* 10.4; *Pol.* 19.6, 15, 23, 29, 49; *Pol.* 20.18; *Pol.* 28.30–32; *Dic.* 1.13.3, 6–8.

12. *Dic.* 1.13.10–18; *Pol.* 1.32–39; *Pol.* 9.21; *Pol.* 18.22; *Pol.* 21.16–19; *Pol.* 38.37.

equity, evil and sinfulness" that every man must know in order to live with himself and with others. He teaches the "actions and omissions that are appropriate to maintaining the public good of human society" as well as the private good of households and families. By the natural law, Althusius wrote in final summary of his position, God "teaches and writes on human hearts the general principles of goodness, equity, evil, and sin, and He instructs, induces, and incites all persons to do good and avoid evil. He likewise condemns the conscience of those who ignore these things and excuses those who do them. He thereby directs them to goodness and dissuades them from evil. If they follow the path of goodness, he excuses them. If they do not, he condemns them."[13]

This natural law has had many names in the classical and Christian traditions, as Althusius recognized: Godly law, divine law, moral law, natural law, natural justice, natural equity, the law of conscience, the law of the mind, the law of reason or right reason, the law inside people, the immutable law, the supreme law, the general law, the common law, and others. Parsing the names for the natural law was not so important to Althusius. He regarded them mostly as synonyms and used them interchangeably.[14]

Knowing the norms that the natural law teaches was the more important and the more difficult task. Althusius knew the traditional formula taught by the medieval scholastics and by the neo-scholastics of his day: that the natural law gives all persons an innate or natural knowledge of good and evil (called *synderesis*), that by exercising their reason persons can come to understand the norms of this natural law, and that by exercising their conscience they can learn to apply these norms equitably to concrete circumstances. However, Althusius also recognized that throughout history persons and peoples have reached different formulations and applications of the natural law. Even in avowed

13. *Dic.* 1.13.1, 14–15; *Pol.* 30.16, 19–20.

14. *Dic.* 1.13.13–18; *Dic.* 1.14; *Pol.* 21.1–20.

Christian societies today, persons have "different degrees of this [natural] knowledge and inclination. This law is not evidently inscribed equally on the hearts of all. The knowledge of it is communicated more abundantly to some and more sparingly to others, according to the will and judgment of God." Thus, given this reality, how can we really know "the nature of the norms of the law that are implanted in us by nature?" How can we be absolutely certain that we as individuals, or as the leaders of our communities, have "a true perception" of the contents of the natural law? How can we even know which person's or community's formulations of the natural law are better than another's. Persons are fallible creatures who perceive natural law only "indirectly," "circumstantially," "through a glass darkly," through "flickering shadows" emitting from distant caves of light. Communities have widely variant "customs, natures, attitudes, and viewpoints" that are affected by the "age, condition, circumstances, and education" of their members. There is no universal code of written natural law to consult. So, how can we be sure of the natural law's norms and contents?[15]

We can know the norms of the natural law if we study both Scripture and tradition, revelation and reason very carefully, Althusius argued. We know that God has given a fuller revelation of his law in the Bible, particularly in the Ten Commandments and in the moral teachings of Moses and the prophets and Christ and the apostles. This cannot be a new form of natural law, for God would not and could not contradict the natural law that he already revealed to all of us in and through our human nature. Biblical moral law is rather a more perfect conformation and elaboration of the natural-law ideas and inclinations that are already inscribed on the hearts and minds of everyone, believers and nonbelievers alike. Through Moses, God rewrote on stone what was already written on our hearts. Through Christ, God rewrote this law anew by fulfilling its commandments and prom-

15. *Dic.* 1.6.4–6, 26; *Dic.* 1.13.16–18; *Pol.* 21.20–21; *Pol.* 23.1–20.

ises and by teaching his followers how to discern its "weightier matters." To be sure, Althusius acknowledged, biblical moral law has clearer precepts and higher purposes than any other form of natural law. It provides a more certain knowledge of the will of God for our lives. It sets out a pathway to salvation for those who can abide by its letter and a pathway to sanctification for those who can live by its spirit. However, the Bible's moral law only rewrites more copiously the natural law that is already written cryptically on the hearts of everyone.[16]

While God and Scripture have rewritten the natural law for believers to discern, reason and experience have rewritten this natural law for nonbelievers to discover. In every major civilization, Althusius argued, enlightened leaders and magistrates have emerged who have used their natural reason to translate the general principles of natural law in their minds into specific positive or proper laws (*leges positivum, leges propriae*) for their communities. These enlightened leaders have inevitably tailored these positive laws to "the customs, nature, needs, attitudes, conditions, and other special circumstances" of the people ruling and being ruled. This has produced widely variant positive laws over time and across cultures, particularly when these local laws are viewed in their details. These enlightened leaders have also inevitably positioned these laws to reflect some of the natural light within their hearts, and have maintained these laws because they have proved to be both right and useful. This has produced laws that are common to many peoples and polities, even those that have had no interaction with each other. Every major civilization, said Althusius, has developed comparable sets of law to govern religious worship and observance, to honor marriage and the family, to obey authorities and to respect traditions, to protect human lives, properties, and reputations, to care for relatives, widows, orphans, and the poor, to speak respectfully to others, to testify truthfully, to honor promises, contracts, and

16. *Pol.* 7.7–12; *Pol.* 10.3–12; *Pol.* 18.32–44; *Pol.* 21.22–29.

agreements, to vindicate wrongs and to punish wrongdoers, to fight wars and repel attacks, to give to each and everyone what is due. These common laws, independently developed by different peoples and polities over time and across cultures, must be regarded as "visible expressions of the same invisible natural law" within all persons, Althusius argued. They must be taken as reflections of "the natural and divine immutable equity that is mixed into them," as indications "of the common practice of natural law."[17]

These common laws (*iura commune*) or laws of nations (*iura gentium*)—gathered from the commonplaces of sundry positive laws and the common practices of sundry legal communities—stand alongside biblical moral laws as a second form and forum of natural law. Indeed, at a certain level of abstraction, the moral laws of the Bible and common laws of the nations converge, even though they have very different origins, ends, and languages. "A law is both natural and common," Althusius wrote, "if the common use of right reason produces it for the necessity and utility of human social life. It, too, can then be called natural law." "While some distinguish among common law (*ius commune*), natural law (*ius naturale*), and the law of nations (*ius gentium*), others more properly call each of them forms of the [same] natural law.... Christ himself often called natural law things that are usually called the law of nations."[18]

This belief in the ultimate concordance, if not confluence, of biblical law, natural law, and common law helps to explain Althusius's somewhat baffling style of argumentation in his *Politics* and *Theory of Justice*. In both tracts, Althusius piled citation upon citation, from all manner of seemingly unrelated sources, in demonstration of each simple assertion about what the natural law contained and commanded. Some of this no doubt was

17. *Dic.* 1.13.4–18; *Dic.* 1.14.1–14; *Dic.* 1.35.22–23; *Pol.* 7.7–12; *Pol.* 9.20–21; *Pol.* 10.3–12; *Pol.* 18.32–44; *Pol.* 21.22–29; *Pol.* 22 passim.

18. *Dic.* 1.13.11, 18–19.

the pedantic puffery of a legal humanist—the flashy displays of unnecessary erudition that still mark some law review articles today. However, for Althusius, all this dense citation to sundry sources evidently had a larger purpose. He seemed convinced that the more frequently a legal teaching and practice appeared in diverse legal, theological, and philosophical texts, the more readily it could be taken as proof of the content of the natural law. If the ancient Israelites directed from Sinai and the ancient Greeks and Romans directed from Olympus independently embraced the same legal teaching, that had to speak volumes about the natural foundations and qualities of this teaching. If Aristotle and Moses, Cicero and Christ, Plato and Paul all concurred on a given principle of right living and proper ruling, that had to give this principle a special priority in discerning the content of natural law. If modern-day Catholics and Protestants, who have been slaughtering and slandering each other with a vengeance, still come to the same conclusions about the cogency and utility of these classical and Christian legal teachings, that had to commend these teachings even more strongly as natural universals. Althusius thus scoured the sources for any and every proof text that he could find to support each step of his argument. This made his writing more of a legal brief than a philosophical argument, more of a historical demonstration of natural-law precepts in action than a logical deduction from *a priori* first principles.[19]

Althusius rested his case on the contents of the natural law most firmly on the confluence between the Commandments of the Decalogue and the moral teachings of sundry classical traditions. For him, the Decalogue was the clearest and most comprehensive confirmation and codification of the natural law, of every person's inner natural inclinations to piety and justice, to faith and order, to love of God and love of neighbor. As such, "the Decalogue has been prescribed for all people to the extent that it agrees with and explains the common law of nature for all

19. *Dic.* 1.14.1–14; *Pol.* 21.30–40; *Pol.* 22.1–3, 10.

peoples." "The precepts of the Decalogue ... infuse a vital spirit into the association and symbiotic life that we teach." "They carry a torch to guide the kind of social life that we desire; they prescribe and constitute a way, rule, guiding star, and boundary for human society. If anyone would take them out of politics, he would destroy it; indeed, he would destroy all symbiosis and social life among men. For what would human life be without the piety of the First Table and the justice of the Second [Table of the Decalogue]? What would a commonwealth be without the communion and communication of things useful and necessary to human life?"[20]

Several times Althusius worked through each of the Commandments to show their enduring natural-law teachings. His formulation in the 1614 *Politics* reads thus:

> The first commandment of the first table is about truly cherishing and choosing God through the knowledge of him handed down in his word, and through unity with him accompanied by a disposition of trust, love, and fear.... The second commandment is about maintaining in spirit and in truth a genuine worship of God through prayers and the use of the means of grace.... The third commandment is about rendering glory to God in all things through the proper use of the names of God, oaths of allegiance to him, respect for what has been created by the Word of God and intercessory prayers.... The fourth commandment is about sanctifying the Sabbath in holy services through hearing, reading, and meditating upon the Word of God.... The fifth commandment is about those things that inferiors are expected to perform toward superiors and vice versa.... The sixth [commandment] requires the defense, protection, and conservation of one's own life and that of one's neighbor. The conservation

20. *Pol.* Preface (1610 and 1614 eds.); *Pol.* 21.29. See further sustained discussions of the Decalogue in *Pol.* 7.7–12; *Pol.* 10.3–12; *Pol.* 18.32–44; *Pol.* 21.22–29, 41; *Dic.* 1.13.10–18; *Dic.* 1.14.1–3; and further brief references in *Pol.* 18.66; *Pol.* 19.14, 31, 59, 69; *Pol.* 27.18; *Pol.* 29.1; *Pol.* 28.32, 38, 77, 100.

> of one's own life comes first, and consists in defense, conservation, and propagation of oneself.... Conservation of the neighbor's life is his protection through friendship and other duties of charity, such as provision for food, clothes, and anything he else needs to be sustained.... The seventh commandment concerns the conservation of one's own mind and body and that of one's neighbor through sobriety, good manners, modesty, discretion, and any other appropriate means... The eighth commandment concerns the defense and conservation of one's goods and those of one's neighbor, and their proper employment in commerce, contracts, and one's vocation.... The ninth commandment concerns the defense and conservation of the good name and reputation of oneself and one's neighbor through honest testimony, just report, and good deed.... The tenth commandment concerns concupiscence, and exerts influence on each of the precepts of the second table. [As Cicero wrote:] "We are taught by the authority and bidding of laws to control our passions, to bridle our every lust, to defend what is ours, and to keep our minds, eyes, and hands from whatever belongs to another."[21]

These moral teachings of the Decalogue are echoed and elaborated elsewhere in the Bible, said Althusius—particularly in the Gospel's repeated explications of the spirit of the Decalogue, and in the many moral lessons set out by the Old Testament prophets and New Testament apostles. These enduring moral laws of the Bible must lie at the foundation of the positive law of any modern Christian polity.

Not all biblical law should be taken as natural law, nor considered mandatory or even useful for our day. Many of the Mosaic laws recorded in the Pentateuch are simply the positive laws of the ancient Jewish people. Many of the legal actions and admonitions of the patriarchs, judges, and kings of ancient Israel are simply evidence of one positive law system in action. Particularly the Mosaic "ceremonial" laws and customs respecting diet,

21. *Pol.* 21.25–27, quoting in part from Cicero, *The Orator*, 1.43.

dress, sacrifice, ritual, levitical life, temple rules, and more, even though authored by God, were specific to the time and place of this ancient wandering tribal people.[22] Christ explicitly rejected the letter of this Mosaic ceremonial law in favor of its general moral spirit. Remember his statement about the complex laws of the Sabbath: "The Sabbath was made for man, not man for the Sabbath" (Mark 2:23–28; Luke 6:1–5). Mosaic ceremonial laws, let alone the later rabbinic accretions upon them, have no place in modern communities—save as an illustration of how one legally sophisticated ancient community exercised its natural inclinations and obligations to religious worship and ritual life. While a modern-day Christian magistrate would do well to develop a comparable set of ceremonial laws tailored to the needs of the local community, and perhaps even emulate some of the ancient biblical prototypes, he cannot simply "impose these Jewish positive laws, which by their nature are changeable and obsolete." That would be to "destroy the Christian liberty" that Christ gave us and to "entangle himself and others in a yoke of slavery."[23]

More useful in our day, for Christian and non-Christian polities alike, are the "juridical laws" of Moses. These are the many detailed laws and procedures set out in the Bible to govern crime and tort, marriage and family, property and commerce, procedure and evidence, and more. These provisions are more useful and probative because they give more specific content, context, and coherence to the Decalogue and other statements of natural law. "[T]he moral commandments of the Decalogue are general," Althusius wrote. "They have no certain, special, and fixed punishment attached to them," let alone procedural mechanisms for how they should be justly and equitably interpreted and applied. The juridical law of Moses "makes more specific

22. See his proto-Montesquieuan insights into the effects of geography on politics in *Pol.* 23.1–14.

23. *Pol.* 21.33–40; *Pol.* 22.3–4; *Dic.* 1.14.5–11; *Dic.* 1.16.9–10; *Dic.* 1.101.43; *Dic.* 1.115.1–36.

determinations, which it relates to the circumstances of the act." So, while the natural law commands "that evildoers ought to be punished," it "proposes nothing concerning the punishment," save the bald commandment, "thou shalt not kill," which does not seem to be just in all circumstances. The juridical law "works out specifically that adulterers, murderers, and the like are to be punished by death, unless the punishment should be mitigated on account of other circumstances. The Mosaic law has various punishments for these crimes," and prescribes a number of useful procedures to weigh the evidence of the crime and to determine a just punishment.[24] Similarly, the Mosaic juridical law offers a number of useful legal rules and procedures for the acquisition, use, and maintenance of public and private property, for the litigation and settlement of private disputes, and for the proper interactions between husband and wife, parent and child, master and servant, creditor and debtor, seller and buyer. None of these juridical positive laws of Moses should be considered binding upon modern day Christians just because they happen to be in the Bible. Insofar as they are parts and products of the natural law, these juridical laws are edifying for our day and can be appropriated as apt in the construction of modern positive laws.[25]

What underscored the natural validity and modern utility of the juridical laws of Moses was that they often had parallels in other legal systems, most notably in classical Roman law. "Virtually all Europeans still use" the classical Roman law, wrote Althusius, because its detailed laws have also proved to be "both right and useful." To be sure, some ancient Roman law provisions betrayed the natural law more than illustrated it. Think of the many old laws celebrating the pagan imperial cult, the domestic laws that permitted infanticide, concubinage, and prostitution, the commercial laws that countenanced exploitation of orphans, captives, slaves, and others. Such laws that openly contradict the

24. *Pol.* 21.33; *Dic.* 1.14.5; *Dic.* 1.16.9–18.

25. *Pol.* 8.72–91; *Pol.* 21.32–33; *Dic.* 1.14.20; *Dic.* 1.15.18–21.

Decalogue and other natural-law principles cannot be viewed as binding on anyone—as the early apostles and church fathers already made clear in their call for legal reforms of Roman society. However, the classical Roman law texts also hold numerous more enlightened legal teachings, many parallel to those in Mosaic juridical law, that are "consistent with the natural law and that cater to public utility and the common good." Some of these Roman laws have also been adopted and adapted into the canon laws of the medieval church and the civil laws of early modern European nations. When these ancient Roman law texts and their later legal adaptations are interpreted and applied "naturally, equitably, and justly," they too can be taken as reflections and illustrations of the natural law in action.[26]

This was the method that Althusius used to work out an elaborate system of public, private, criminal, and procedural law for his day. He started with the natural-law principles of Scripture and tradition. He then cited the elaboration of these principles in the precepts and procedures of various legal systems with an eye to discovering and demonstrating what they held in common. He combed very carefully through biblical law and classical Roman law. He rummaged more freely and selectively through medieval and early modern civil law, canon law, feudal law, manorial law, and urban law. Althusius's method was not always so neat or cogent. Sometimes he repeated his discussion of the same natural-law principle or precept in different chapters and books, with each discussion somewhat different from the

26. *Dic.* 1.14.1–20; *Dic.* 1.15.1–21; *Dic.* 1.16.8; *Pol.* 8.72–86; *Pol.* 21.30–40; *Pol.* 22.1–3, 10. An important Calvinist prototype for this theory of the Mosaic juridical laws on which Althusius evidently drew was that of Theodore Beza, Calvin's handpicked successor in Geneva. Trained in law, Beza developed an interesting account of how the Mosaic juridical laws compared with those of Roman law. In his *Lex Dei, moralis, ceremonialis et politica* (Geneva, 1577), Beza used Roman law categories to arrange his collection of these juridical laws. I am grateful to Professor Christoph Strohm for alerting me to this tract.

last. Sometimes he just dumped into one long string citation all kinds of passages whose intersection with each other, let alone integration with the natural-law principle in question, was not obvious. Sometimes he would pluck out one ancient passage as normative, even when many other passages in the same source qualified or contradicted the one he singled out. Sometimes he would just arbitrarily pick a provision from Mosaic, civil, or canon law and declare it to be a provision of the common law of nations, without showing its analogues in other legal systems. There was more *a priori* reasoning at work in Althusius's theory than he let on. However, these caveats aside, his demonstrative method of argument produced an astonishingly comprehensive and complex jurisprudence.

An Illustration of Natural Rights

Althusius used this demonstrative method to work out a detailed account of all manner of legal subjects—conscience and commandment, contracts and covenants, procedure and evidence, advocacy and appeal, marriage and family, corporations and associations, business and commerce, torts and crimes, property and poverty, rights and liberties, privileges and immunities, federalism and constitutionalism, and so forth.

Let me illustrate how he used this method to develop one legal subject—the "freedom and rights of the body" (*libertas et iura corporis*). Both in his *Politics* and in his *Theory of Justice*, Althusius presented this as a natural right, anchored in the Commandment, "Thou shalt not kill," and its echoes in a number of Greek and Roman legal and philosophical texts.[27] In his *Theory of Justice*, he went on to "demonstrate" what this bodily freedom entailed. His most thorough discussion came in two chapters on "freedom and its characteristics." These chapters were wedged between long

27. *Pol.* 7.9–10; *Pol.* 10.5–6; *Pol.* 21.27; *Dic.* 1.25.7; *Dic.* 1.106.1–4; *Dic.* 1.117.1–2, 6, 17–24.

chapters on the legal power of a master over his slaves and of a paterfamilias over his household. Althusius seemed to position his freedom discussion to underscore the natural limits that even a master and father had to respect, despite the repeated admonitions of natural, biblical, and Roman law alike that these authorities be "honored, respected, and obeyed."

Althusius's opening passage on the right to bodily freedom reads thus:

> There is a freedom of the body by which the civil law allows a person to use his bodily members to do or conduct anything in a way that is both agreeable and permissible. This is given to us as a natural right, unless obvious exceptions are made.[28]

Althusius cited six texts from Justinian's *Corpus Iuris Civilis* to support this proposition. He started with a text from Justinian's *Institutes*, which gave an expansive definition of the rights of "freedmen" in ancient Rome. "Freedom, from which the expression freedmen is derived, is the natural ability to do anything one wishes, unless it is prohibited by force or by law."[29] He next cited a text from Justinian's *Digest* that gave the same definition of liberty, but now without restricting it to "freedmen" and while condemning slavery as "an institution of the *ius gentium*, whereby someone, contrary to nature, is made subject to the ownership of another."[30] A couple of sentences later Althusius lifted up several other Roman law texts that countenanced the emancipation of slaves, servants, captives, and children, and expanded the category and liberties of "freedmen" and free born citizens.[31] The upshot of these texts was that freedom is a natural and native quality of all men, and those who are not free should be made free as far as possible. As he later put it: "Today, all freed-

---

28. *Dic.* 1.25.7. See also *Dic.* 1.117.6.

29. Justinian, *Institutes*, 1.3. See also *Pol.* 38.8.

30. Justinian, *Digest*, 1.5.4.

31. Justinian, *Institutes*, 1.3, 5; 2.1, 12, 15.

men have become completely free."[32] But lest the reader think that Roman law countenanced outright hedonism in its call for "freedom of each to do whatever he wishes" up to the limits of the law, Althusius pointed to two other texts from the *Digest* that counseled virtuous exercise of freedom: "Not everything which is lawful is honorable." And with respect to freedom of the body in marriage: "In such unions, one must always consider not only what is lawful but what is honorable."[33]

Alongside these classical Roman law texts, Althusius lined up a dozen biblical passages that made similar points. He contrasted the natural freedom that all should enjoy with the unnatural slavery imposed by enemies or family members. Ignoring the many other Old Testament passages on slavery, he pointed to Deuteronomy 20:11 as a warning against slavery and servitude: "If they accept and open their gates, all the people in it shall be subject to forced labor and shall work for you." He also cited the Apocryphal book Sirach 33:20 that extended this call for freedom to the household: "Let neither son nor wife, neither brother nor friend, have power over you as long as you live." Again to avoid the seeming hedonism of these passages, he pointed to several passages from Saint Paul that echoed the Roman law texts in their calls for prudence. He included 1 Corinthians 6:12: "Everything is permissible for me, but not everything is beneficial." Also 1 Corinthians 8:9: "Be careful, however, that the exercise of your freedom does not become a stumbling block to the weak."

Althusius went on to describe the bodily freedom taught by the natural law as follows:

> It is the power to make law or to disregard it, to choose to release one's own business when it is in need of management. It is [to have] bodily freedom, or the very uninhibited use of one's body, a freedom of nature or of action, the opposite of

32. *Dic.* 1.25.30.

33. Justinian, *Digest*, 50.17.144, 197.

> which is imprisonment, confinement, bondage and chains. [It is freedom] to use one's own, or another's, as appropriate.[34]

In support of these propositions, Althusius cited two dozen passages from the *Corpus Iuris Civilis* and from a modern commentary thereon by Antoine Favre. He included several titles in the *Institutes* and *Digest* on "the rights of persons" (*iura personae*) in general, and the rights of "free born persons," "freedmen," and "manumitted" and "emancipated" slaves, servants, and children. He also included a number of passages on specific rights and freedoms respecting marriage and family life, the acquisition and use of property and business interests, and their alienation by contract, gift, or testament. He again made clear, citing Justinian's *Code*, that the "status of freedman," while highly coveted, does "not afford an exemption from civil duties," nor release a person from his or her "natural obligations."[35]

Althusius intermixed with these Roman law texts ten biblical passages that added further nuance and balance. For example, he supported the natural freedom "to make one's own law or to disregard it" and to have "uninhibited use of one's body" with a citation to the cautions of 1 Corinthians 7:4–6: "The wife's body does not belong to her alone but also to her husband. In the same way, the husband's body does not belong to him alone but also to his wife. Do not deprive each other except by mutual consent." He added to the list Ephesians 5:29 that underscored Saint Paul's teaching that one's body is to be preserved as a "temple of the Lord": "After all, no one ever hated his own body, but he feeds and cares for it, just as Christ does the Church." Likewise, he supported the proposition that the person has the natural right to make use of his own or another's property with citations to Genesis 50:5–6 and Jeremiah 40:1–3, among others, which taught

34. *Dic.* 1.25.7. For crimes and torts against this bodily freedom, see *Dic.* 1.117.

35. Justinian, *Institutes*, 1.3–6, 9; 2.1; 3.8–9; Justinian, *Digest*, 1.5, 7; 28.1–31; 50.16.10–11; 50.17.4–15, 118, 144, 197; Justinian, *Code*, 6.37.

that all such property uses need to respect the basic natural-law duties to love God, neighbor, and self. The lesson in this cluster of passages was clear: freedom of the body and its support is a natural good, but it must be exercised with due moderation and respect for virtue and for the interests of others.

A few pages later in the *Theory of Justice*, Althusius returned to his exposition of the freedom of the body, now with attention to the doctrine of self-defense and defense of others:

> The protection of one's body and life is how nature makes a man's body free. This is within his power and character. He has the freedom to use and care for his own limbs, and this is invaluable. For this reason, the law allows any man the protection, defense, and preservation of his body and life from harm. Thus he is allowed to carry weapons. He is to be free and immune from murder, assault, beating, whipping, wounds, punishment, mutilation, lashing, attack, branding, and any other sort of abuse, punishment, imprisonment, repression or detainment. He is to be free from all injustice, cruelty, and improper coercion.
>
> The protection of one's life and body are natural human properties. This is considered the most important thing. Accordingly, a man is given the right to protect himself against force and injury, and he is similarly allowed to use harshness and force against those injuring him or bringing force to bear against him. This defense extends first to one's person and life, and then to everything that serves the interests of the human body and life, such as the value of his reputation, goods, and relatives.
>
> While one is permitted to repel and turn aside force, this cannot be done by killing when one is inflicted only by a light wound or when there is only a slight danger to one's life given the type of weapon, assailant, struggle, or blow. But a man may certainly resist with deadly force an attack inflicted upon his body. And he may defend a strong attack against him with equal strength … so long as the defensive force is not greater or fiercer than the attacking force. The protection of one's dignity and reputation against harm or

> provocation, however, should not be made with force but only with words.
>
> The features and benefits of this protection are that it is permitted to resist a thief or an attacker or anyone using force to ensure one's own safety. The protection of family members and domestic servants is also allowed.[36]

Embedded in this discussion were citations to nearly one hundred texts from the Bible and Apocrypha, many of them specific provisions and examples of proper protection of one's life, liberty, property and family drawn from the Mosaic law of crime and tort and the glosses thereon by Christ and St. Paul—though Althusius ducked the hard Gospel passages where Christ called his followers "to turn the other cheek" (Matt. 5:39; Luke 6:29). Interwoven with these biblical passages were nearly fifty passages from the classical Roman law, particularly the *lex Aquilia*, and various glosses and commentaries on these Roman law texts by Catholic and Protestant jurists—Benedict Aretius, Julius Clarus, Diego Covarruvias, Andreas Gail, Joseph Mascardus, Jacob Menochius, Fernando Vásquez, and Matthaeus Wesembecke.

Thus Althusius went on—piling passage upon passage, proof text upon proof text to demonstrate the concordance that he saw between biblical and rational, classical and Christian, Catholic and Protestant forms and formulations of natural-law principles. One can almost see him sitting in the library for many months on end poring over huge piles of legal and theological texts and compiling massive lists of each and every passage that he could find that bore on a given topic. Once he completed his reading, he must have just divided and subdivided these lists into ever more discrete categories, following his favorite Ramist techniques, and then inserted these lists of citations at apt points throughout his own text. It is an utterly fascinating and utterly exhausting display of erudition.

---

36. *Dic.* 1.26.21–27. See further *Dic.* 1.106.1–4.

This was not just idle pedantry, however. Althusius was writing for a world that was wracked by the inquisition and by religious warfare between and among Protestants and Catholics. He was writing for a fragile Netherlands that was still struggling to create a coherent nation-state after its bloody revolt from Spain. He was writing for a Holy Roman Empire, a vast archipelago of 350 polities, each bent on preserving its own fragile rights and liberties. His natural-law theory was designed to produce a new concordance of discordant canons that transcended differences of creed, country, and custom. This was a Calvinist theory in its origins but it was universal in its orientation and ambition.

Inevitably, Althusius's universal theory of law was a creature of his time, and his legal ken was conditioned by the legal sources at his disposal. It is remarkable to me how fresh and vital his legal insights remain for our day. Furthermore, it is tempting to try out Althusius's "demonstrative theory" with a wider set of legal texts before us—not just texts from the classical, Jewish, and Christian West, but legal texts from all the axial religions around the world, including Islam, Hinduism, Buddhism, Confucianism, and more. This "demonstrative method" might well show the world today that, despite our bitter culture wars and bloody military battles, there is a great deal more confluence than conflict in our fundamental legal teachings and practices. Indeed, developing a new world concordance of discordant canons might well hold far greater promise for peace and order than negotiating yet another transient treaty or temporary truce.

On

Law and Power

PREFACE*

To those highly distinguished—eminent in virtue, knowledge, and position—illustrious and wise men, the lord consuls and senators of the illustrious city of Emden, those lords who most deserve my respect,

Greetings.

My highly distinguished, wise, illustrious, and experienced lords who deserve my respect, a few years ago I published my *Roman Jurisprudence*. This treatise has been praised and attacked at different times in different places contrary to my thoughts and anticipations. In addition, other learned and eminent men have advised me a number of times to recall that treatise so that I might iron out and explain more fully what I expressed rather succinctly, briefly, and obscurely. Diligently have I obeyed my advisors, and whatever leisure time I have had away from my

* Translated from Johannes Althusius, *Dicaeologicae libri tres, Totum & universum Jus, quo utimur methodice complectentes* (Frankfurt: Corvinus, 1649). Althusius's reference apparatus has been faithfully rendered as endnotes, with the original text in italics.

duties and obligation to the state I devoted to this concern and pursuit. These earlier concerns have produced a work that is almost completely new and is, in fact, different in many ways from the previous one. I had intended to help those studying my *Jurisprudence* with the talent that God has given to me. If I have attained this goal, let me give thanks to God because it is he who gave me the strength. If not, at the very least, I have given others an opportunity to think more fully about these matters. I have recalled the legal material, scattered in the books of the *Corpus Juris Civilis*, by specific chapters and headings. What has been blown and scattered by some from their proper abodes I have returned to their own proper places and put in order. I have arranged all the topics according to my own judgment by their logical succession and explication so that by their sequence they may cast light on the following discussions and later discussions may receive illumination from the earlier ones. Some topics used to wander, ramble, and stray into grey areas, where some require them to be under the headings of possession or ownership, others under agreements, others under private wrongdoings, others under criminal trials, and still others assign them to their own separate category. In fact, some topics until now were banished, driven from the boundaries of the judicial realm as if they were exiles (απολιδες) legally unworthy of juridical citizenship. To these I have granted their possessions, which had been seized with injury. I have returned them to their own homes, and I have restored them to their own families. In all these instances, I have used the freedom of my own judgment, leaving the same freedom to others. For you, however, my exalted, most distinguished and revered lords, I believe that I have justly written down these labors of mine. Indeed, they were born in your realm, and they rightly recognize you as patrons because God has gathered for you the keys of this city, which is the center of all of Frisia. In this way, my work may proclaim the kindness you have shown to me, your favor, and the goodwill with which you have attended me for the many years in which I have served your illustrious state. In addition, the material that is treated in this book is, for the most part, familiar to you and commonplace, and it seems to require such patrons as you, that is, just and active ones. You yourselves, I say, are the ones who governed this most populous state during such difficult, dangerous, and disastrous times while you oversaw the Belgic Wars with great strength, courage, and outstanding prudence with God as your confidence and leader. Not only have you steered the Republic's fleet through such serious and dangerous gusts of storms—driven and beaten as it was by force of wind and flow of water—to a safe port, but also, because of your exceptional and outstanding policies by which it is possible for certain cities to battle with empires, you have provided for it, enriched it, and protected it with God's blessing from the violence, attacks, and activities of our enemies, both foreign and domestic, as well as the many grumblers and complainers. Therefore, most distinguished, illustrious, and wise men, receive this gift as a testament of your kindness to me and my love for you and as a pledge for the duty by which I am bound to your state. May God protect the state in this uncertain region from rebellion, fear, and revolution; may he keep your church, and all who profess Christ, flourishing; and may he keep you safe as long as possible. May he rule with a spirit of wisdom and strength everywhere. May he advance and enrich his blessing in a greater and greater way.

Emden on the Kalends of March 1618
Most Favorably Yours,
Johannes Althusius

Book 1, Chapter 13

On Common Law

Up to this point, in the first section of the *Dicaeologicae*, I have discussed agreements; in the next section, I will discuss law.[1]

1. What Law Is — In my opinion, law is this:[2] something that is established after coming into being because of an action[3] in a human[4] affair,[5] or because of some individual,[6] for the necessity, benefit,[7] and direction of this life.[8]

2. Its Different Titles — For this reason, law publicly or privately is usefully called[9] an establishment for the good of humanity;[10] a precept concerning an agreement between individuals;[11] a regulation of just and unjust things; a regulation of the just and unjust; a governor, a leader of the good; an oral agreement of the state;[12] a norm for behavior and a way of life;[13] the distinguisher of the just and unjust;[14] a bill of works, that is, things that must be done;[15] a statute; judgment; bill;[16] and the rule of justice.[17]

3. The Establishment and Types of Law — In the definition of law that I have provided, I have included its establishment and different forms.[18]

4. The Reason for Law — Law is established when something, because of the nature and quality of an individual agreement, according to right reason,[19] as required by human welfare and necessity,[20] is conceived and implemented.[21]

5. Law Arising from an Action — Therefore, it is said about law that an individual judgment must proceed from an action,[22] and I, as I peruse this topic in Justinian's *Juris Civilis*, respond in accordance with the things that were said there.[23] Also, it is asked what is the kind of law arising from an action;[24] the intention behind the action;[25] the case in which the law is settled;[26] and the situation from which it is established,[27] that is, what the action or agreement was when the circumstances and parties are well known.[28] Thus, an action that is accompanied by no law is naked or bare.[29] Today, legal experts call this law the essential point of litigation. As for which law is limited,[30] what is applicable and what is subjected[31] and what law is not under the authority of judges,[32] the *Juris Civilis* usually answers these questions for those who are interested.[33] Among Jewish lawyers, even [Moses], the lawgiver himself, renders judgments concerning the law.[34]

6. The Structure of Law — The structure of law is twofold—natural or common law and civil or individual law[35]—just as the welfare and necessity of human life that law protects is twofold: common to all or appropriate to individual places and people.

7. The Nature of Natural Law — A law is natural and common if common right reason produces it for the common necessity and welfare of human social life in general. Therefore, it is called natural law.

8. The Nature of Civil Law — A law is civil or individual if individual right reason introduces and establishes it because of the necessity and welfare of the social life of some specific place. Therefore, it is called individual law or the civil law of some place.

9. A Common Error — The types of law are incorrectly defined by common people as common law, natural law, the law of nations, and civil law. In fact, they are not types, that is, effects of law, but they are the efficient causes. According to Justinian, all law that has been compiled comes from these precepts of natural and right reason.[36]

10. Necessity and the Common Good as Reasons for the Establishment of Law — These come from the reasoning of the welfare and necessity of human life.[37] Because of these efficient causes of nature, a community, or some specific place, law is called natural law, the law of nations, or civil law—that is, law common to all people or the law of an individual population.[38] In another place[39] it is even called natural justice or civil justice.[40] It is also called natural law or proper law.[41]

11. Common Law — Therefore, common law is that which has been inscribed on human hearts by nature or by God from birth and that by which human beings are moved either to act or avoid actions, whichever is sufficient for preserving the common good of human society, convicts wrongdoers of evil, or excuses the innocent.[42]

12. The Knowledge of and Tendency toward Natural Law in Human Beings — Thus, there is a knowledge and natural inclination for this law in the human heart. Because of it, a person knows what is just and is urged by the hidden impulse of nature to do what is just and to not do what is unjust.[43]

13. Different Terms for Natural Law — This law is designated with different names. Sometimes it is called natural law.[44] Other times, it is called the law of nature.[45] It is also called natural reason,[46] the silent law,[47] the law that nature provides to the human race,[48] the rule or law of God,[49] or the immutable law.[50]

14. Where the Foundations of Law Lie — Moreover, God teaches and inscribes on human hearts general principles of fairness and justice and unfairness and injustice; he binds, urges, and incites all people either to do or avoid these things; and by means of their internal consciences he accuses those who fail in these things and excuses those who do them.[51] Therefore, he urges people toward good and calls them back from evil. If someone follows his leading to good, that person is excused. Whoever does not, he accuses.

15. Duties Arising from Natural Law — The principles that I mentioned above concern the two primary duties human beings have. The first involves ourselves; the second involves others.

With respect to ourselves, there are three main impulses: (1) self-defense, (2) self-preservation, and (3) self-propagation.

For discussions concerning self-defense, especially our defense against violence and injury, see the sources cited.[52]

As to self-preservation and the protection of each individual's own property, see the texts noted below.[53]

Self-propagation includes both the union of men and women[54] and the proper rearing of the children born to us.[55]

A duty shown to another looks either to God or our neighbor.

It looks to God, who truly teaches and inscribes this law, to the extent that it teaches us and urges us to the knowledge and worship of him,[56] for which reason it also looks to the first table of the Decalogue.[57]

It looks to our neighbor to the extent that it teaches and excites us to the duties of protecting our neighbors and avoiding the injuring of them, for which reason it looks to the second table of the Decalogue.[58] Third, it teaches us that whatever you wish to be done to you, you should also do to another, and the converse.[59] This means to live righteously, to not hurt another, and to give to each person what is owed.[60]

16. The Degrees and Limits of Natural Knowledge and Tendencies — Moreover, although those principles of nature are one and the same to all nations, still they differ in the level and means of their inscribing and urging. In fact, these principles are not equally inscribed on the hearts of all; in some, they are inscribed more eloquently, abundantly, and effectively, while in others not eloquently, but sparingly, according to God's will for inscribing and teaching. Therefore, it is the case that although these principles have been written on everyone's heart, nevertheless the conclusions that are drawn from them are not equally held. Instead, some people understand how to infer more conclusions from them, others fewer. In addition, natural reason often is deluded both with respect to the understanding of the ideas of these shared principles present in the mind—since it does not understand them lucidly and clearly enough in each and every thing—and with respect to the manipulation of the individual ideas, the conclusions drawn from the common principles, and the application to individual affairs in which reason's ability and will is weak, differs, and often disagrees with itself.[61]

17. The Degrees and Limits of Natural Knowledge and Tendencies — The means and level of the urging and exciting to do these things that are taught by those principles also varies. In fact, many people very carelessly disdain those things that are known from natural law.[62] Others are more effectively instigated to observe them as they concentrate upon the study of these principles. Clearly, in the hearts of the elect, this law of nature is always more eloquent and effective, just as God promised.[63]

18. The Distinctions Others Have Made Between Natural Law and the Law of Nations — This common law others divide into natural law and law of nations.[64] It is a little better in other places.[65] Others, in fact, call each by its correct title, natural.[66] Natural law applies to human beings alone and that which is named law of nations often is called natural law in the *Juris Civilis*.[67] What they call natural law is described as what simple intellectual reason without proof (ἀναπόδεικτος) teaches human beings, in as much as they are humans and rational creatures,[68] in order that they should live holy and blameless lives.[69] For this reason, it is called by some rational law[70] or innate law,[71] although this very law does not arise exclusively for itself but is only a notion (ἔννοια), the knowledge of which—or rather the ability to understand this law—arises from nature. Thus, it is also called natural law[72] or it could be called natural justice[73] because brute animals sometimes imitate this law and are said to have some appearances of it.[74]

19. The Law of Nations — In their opinion, the law of nations is whatever is enacted through demonstration, calm reasoning, or a discourse of the mind, by a human being, who cultivates animal instinct, political society, and the human good,[75] so that in this common human life we may live good, happy, and pleasant lives.[76] It is in this spirit that the apostle commands us to be beneficial to other people.[77]

It teaches us to live well and have pleasant lives because it establishes what is beneficial and necessary for human life,[78] and because it is adapted to human society.[79] Here, the reflection of law seen in animals is not visible.[80]

20. Its Different Titles for the Law of Nations — This law of nations Justinian sometimes calls natural law, sometimes benefit,[81] something received for the sake of utility,[82] better justice,[83] good justice,[84] pure law of nations,[85] against nature or natural reason,[86] or even law established out of fairness through convincing logic.[87] Wesenbeck[88] calls it the law of reasoning.

21. Examples — From this law wars are conducted, the treatment of captives and the punishment of criminals are decided, most contracts are disputed, the distinctions of personal property are made, and judicial decisions are rendered, kingdoms and cities are established, and magistracies are enacted.[89] In short, similar necessities and benefits are established for the continuation and conservation of human society.[90]

Notes

1. *vide supra cap 1. num 4.*

2. *Nam alias varias habet significationes, de quibus in l. pen. & ult. de just. & jur. l. 2. de bis qui sunt sui, vel alien. jur. l. jura. de reg. jur. l. 23 de adopt. §. ult. Instit. de legit. agnat. success. in princ. Inst. de reb. corpor. & incorp l. 4. de suis & legit. hared. l. 25. de verb. sign. §. ult. Inst. de poena temere litigant. Cujac. in l. 1. de just. & jure. Donell. lib. 1. com. c. 3.*

3. *l. 52. §. 2. ad L. Aquil. l. 1. §. 3. ad L. Cornel. de sicar. l. 3. quod vi aut clam. l. 9. §. 1. quod fals. tut. l. 52. de obligat. & action. l. 11. §. 12. de adulter. l. 10. in fin. de cap. minut. l. 16. de stat. hom. l. 30. de test. tut. l. 52. pro soc. l. 79. §. 1. de judic. argum. Exod. c. 18.*

15.16 & seqq. 1. Corinth. cap. 6. 2.3.4.5.6. Deut. cap. 17. per tot. vide supra c. 1. num. 8.

4. *§. ult. Inst. de jur. person. l. 2. de stat. hom. l. 28. de usur. Genes. cap. 1. 26.28. Psalm 8.*

5. *argum. §. ult. Instit. de jure nat. gent. & civili.*

6. *l. 1. de stat. hom. l. 3. de oblig. & actio.*

7. *1. Corinth. c. 6. 3.4 c. 7. 31.39.30. §. 1. Inst. de oblig. quae ex quasi cont. §. 10. Instit. de mandat. §. 2. Instit. de jure nat. gent. & civili.*

8. *Exod. c. 18. 20. & seqq. Proverb. c. 6. 23.*

9. *l. 1. §. hujus. l. pen. de just. & jure. l. 2. §. 1. de origin. jur. l. 2. de constit. pr. l. 25. de legib. Siracid. c. 4. 4. & seqq. ut i Junius. Mich. c. 6. 8. 1. Timoth. c. 2. 1.2.3.4. 1. Corinth. c. 12. 7. & seqq. 2. Coloss. c. 1. 10. Deut. c. 12. 10.*

10. *d l. 2. de stat. hom. §. ult. Instit. de jure nat. gent. l. 28. de usur.*

11. *Exod. c. 18. 16.22.26. c. 22. 9. Deut. cap. 17. 8.9. & seqq. 1. Thess. c. 4. 6. Act. c. 19. 38.*

12. *l. 1. l. 2. de legib. Exod. c. 18. 16. & seqq.*

13. *d. c. 18. 20. & seqq. Prov. c. 6. 23.*

14. *§. 1. Instit. de just. & jure. l. 10. D. d. t. Heb. c. 5. 14. Philip. c. 1. 9.10. arg. 1. Corinth. c. 12. 9. 1. Joh. c. 4. 1.*

15. *Rom. c. 3. 27. Matth. c. 23. 23. c. 11. 42.*

16. *Deut. c. 17. 9. & seqq. Prov. c. 6. 23. Exod. c. 18. 16.20. 2. Chron. c. 19. 8.9.10.11. Psal. 119. per tot.*

17. *Rom. c. 9. 31. c. 6. 19. Matth. c. 6. 1. 33. Tit. c. 2. 12. Jacob. c. 1. 20.*

18. *Consentit Hilliger. lib. 1. c. 2. & lib. 2. c. 1. Donell. enucleat. de speciebus juris. vide infra cap. 18. num. 1. 2.*

19. *l. 9. ibi, naturalis ratio. de just. & jur.*

20. *§. 2. ibi, nam usu, &c. Inst. de jur. nat. gent. & civ.*

21. *§. ult. Inst. de just. & jur. l. 1. §. 2. D. d. t.*

22. *l. 15. de transact. l. creditor. §. 4. qui potior. in pign. 2. Sam. c. 12. 1. 2. & seqq. 1. Reg. c. 3. 16.17. c. 20. 39.40.41. Num. c. 15. 32. & seqq. Jos. c. 7. 20.21 & seqq. Exod. c. 18. 16.17.18. Num. c. 16. c. 27. 2.3.4. Matth. c. 26. 61. & seqq. c. 21. 33.34.35.40.41. Esth. c. 1. 13.14. & seqq. Act. c. 5. 1.2. & seqq. 1. Reg. c. 20. 39.40.41.42.*

23. *l. 49. de vulg. substit. l. 11. l. 69. de hered. instit. Ant. Faber jurispr. tit. 1. illat. 7.*

24. *l. 28. de usu & usufr. legat. l. 30. de test. tutel. l. 7. §. ult. de distract. pign. l. 114. §. apud. de legat. 1. l. 15. de manum. vindict. l. 8. §. illud. quib. mod. pign. vel hypoth. l. 80. ad L. Falcid. l. 41. de reb. cred. l. 19. qui test. fac. poss. l. 31. §. ult. de mort. caus. donas. l. 7. qui satisd. cogant.*

25. *l. 5. §. 1. de divers. & temp. praescript. l. 35. de hared. instit.*

26. *l. 52. §. 7. ad L. Aquil.*

27. *l. 1. §. 3. ad L. Cornel. de sicar.*

28. *l. 16. de poen. l. 14. de divers. & temp. praescript. l. 3. §. 2. de testib. l. 12. §. 2. rem rat. hab. l. 51. §. 2. l. 48. ad L. Aquil.*

29. *l. 48. §. de solut. l. 3. l. 9 §. 5. de adquir. rer. dom. l. 52. §. 1. l. 2. de verb. obligat.*

30. *l. 2. de jur. & fact. ignorant. l. 9. l. 10 & seqq. de legib.*

31. *l. 1. l. 9. §. 3. de juris & fact. ignor. l. 2. §. 43. de origin. jur. l. 10. de bonor. possess.*

32. *l. 15. §. 1. ad munic. l. 1. §. 1. ad SC. Turpill. Deut. c. 17. 7.8.9.10. & seqq.*

33. *l. 79. de judic. l. 16. de stat. hom. vide infr. cap. 15.*

34. *Exod. c. 18. 15. & seqq. Deut. c. 1. 16.17. cap. 17. 2.3.4.5. & seqq. 2. Chron. c. 19. de quae re d. cap. 15.*

35. *arg. §. ult. Instit. de just. & jur. l. 1. §. 2. D. d. tit.*

36. *§. ult. Inst. de just. & jur. l. 1. §. 2. D. eod.*

37. *§. 2. ibi, nam usu exigente & humanis necessitatibus gentes humanae quaedam jura sibi constituerunt. Instit. de jur. nat. gent. & civil. §. 1. ibi, nam quod quisque populus sibi jus constituit. §. 11. ibi, quae ipsa quaeque sibi civitas constituit. §. 4. 5. 6. Inst. d. tit. textus elegans in l. 9. omnes. l. pen. de just. & jur. l. 64. de constit. pre. l. 5. l. 16. de legib. l. 2. de const. princ.*

38. *l. 6. l. 9. l. pen. de just. & jur. §. 1.2.3. Instit. de jur. nat. gent. & civil. l. 1. de adq. rer. dom. l. 195. de verb. sign. l. 16. de minor. l. ult. C. de in integr. rest. minor. §. sacrum 7. Inst. de nupt. §. 1. Inst. de milit. testam. l. 51. §. pen. de fidejuss. l. ult. C. de in integr. restit. min. §. 3. §. fin. Instit. quib. non est permiss. test. cond.*

39. *Cujac. lib. 15. obs. c. 33.*

40. *l. 1. §. 1. si quis test. lib. esse juss. l. 45. §. qui cum. ad L. Aquil. §. retinenda. Inst. de interdict. §. ult. de superficieb. l. 39. de negot. gest. l. 1. de contrar. tut. act. l. 31. deposit. vid. Connan. lib. 1. com. c. 3. c. 4.*

41. *§. 14. sed cum ea. Inst. de hared. quae ab intestat. §. 7. Inst. de usu & habitat. l. 77. de reg. jur. tit. Inst. de legit. agnat. tutel. tit. de legit. hared. l. 6. de pact.*

42. *ad Rom. c. 1. 19.20.21.32. cap. 2.15.16.17. 1. Corinth. c. 5. 1.2.3. c. 11. 14.*

43. *Roman. cap. 2. 15.16. c. 7. 22.23.15.16.17.18.*

44. *tit. Inst. de jure natur. gent. & civ.*

45. *§. 1. Instit. de jur. nat. gent. l. penult. de justit. & jure. §. singulorum. §. res vendita. Institut. de rer. divis. l. 16. §. naturales. de fidejuss. l. 10. de obligat. & actio. l. 95. §. natura. de solus. l. 126. §. Chrysogonus. de verb. obligat. l. 16. §. 4. de minor. l. 22. locat.*

46. *§. 1. Instit. de jur. natur. gent. l. 9. l. 1. §. 3. l. 6. l. 11. de just. & jur. l. 1. de adquir. rer. dom. l. 1. de minor. l. 7. §. 1. de integr. restit. §. 12. fera. Instit. de rer. divis. l. 1. l. 2. l. 14. l. 15. l. 16. de legib. 1. Cor. c. 11. 13.14. Rom. c. 2. 16.*

47. *l. cum ratio 7. de bon. damnat.*

48. *§. 11. singulorum. §. 41. vendita. Instit. de rer. divis. l. 1. de adquir. rer. dom. jus gentium. d. §. 11. l. 9. de just. & jur. Donell. lib. 1. comm. c. 6.*

49. *Rom. c. 1. 32. c. 2. c. 7. 22.25.*

50. *Rom. c. 2. 16. Esa. c. 49. 15. Matth. c. 14. 4.5.7.9. §. pen. ubi Dd. Instit. de jur. nat. gent. & civili.*

51. *Rom. c. 2. 15.16. c. 7. 22.23. & v. 15.16.17.18.*

52. *l. 4. l. 5. ad L. Aquil. l. 1. C. und. vi. l. 3. de just. & jur. vide Zoanett. de defens. triplici. part. 1.*

53. *Ephes. c. 5. 29. Coloss. c. 2. in fin. Siracid. c. 14. 4.5.6.7.8.9.10. c. 23. 21. c. 30. 26.*

54. *l. 1. §. pen. de just. & jur. §. 1. 2. Instit. de jur. nat. gent. & civil.*

55. *d. loc. & tit. de agnosc. & alend. lib.*

56. *Rom. c. 1. 19.20.21. Zanchius de lege natur. lib. 1. c. 10.*

57. *Matth. c. 22. 36.37.38.39.40. Luc. c. 10. 27.*

58. *Matth. & Luc. d. locis.*

59. *Matth. c. 7. 2.12. Luc. c. 13. 14. Lev. cap. 19.18. Rom. c. 2. 13.21.22. 1. Johan. c. 2. 11. tit. quod quisque juris in al. arg. Esai. c. 58. 7. 1. Joh. c. 3. 15. c. 4. 20.21.*

60. *§. juris. Inst. de just. & jur. l. 10. §. 1. eod. Rom. c. 12. 9.17. & seqq. c. 13. 7.8. 1. Timoth. c. 2. 2. Matth. c. 22. 17.21. Exod. c. 22. 22.23.24. Marc. c. 12. 16.17. 1. Thess. c. 4. 12. c. 5. 22.*

61. *Rom. c. 7. 15.16.17.18.19.20.21.22.23. 1. Cor. cap. 2. 10.11. & seqq. Jerem. c. 17. Johan. c. 3. Genes. c. 8.*

62. *arg. Rom. c. 7. 22.23.25. & seqq. Psalm. 10. 4. Psalm. 36. 2. Rom. c. 1. 24.28. 1. Timoth. cap. 4. 2.*

63. *Jerem. c. 31.*

64. *Ulpian in l. 1. de adquir. rer. dom. l. 1. §. 3. 4. l. 6 de just. & jure. §. 3. Instit. d. t. & tit. Instit. de jure natur. gent. & civil.*

65. *Cujac. in l. 1. §. hujus. de just. & jure. & lib. 15. obs. c. 33.*

66. *per §. 11. singulorum. & seq. & §. 41. vendita. Instit. de rer. divis. l. 31. deposit. Donell. lib. 1. com. c. 6. Eguin. Baro. Instit. de jure natur. gent. & civil. & Apostolus ad Rom. c. 1. & 2. & 1. Corinth. c. 11. 14. & cap. 5. 1.2.*

67. *l. 1. §. ult. l. seq. l. 9. de just & jur. l. naturales 10. de obligat. & actio. l. 65. §. natura. de solut. l. 31. l. 1. de adquir. rer. dom. l. 84. §. 1. de reg. jur. §. 11 & seqq. §. 20. §. 29. §. 40. §. 41. Instit. de. rer. divis. Anton. Faber jurisprud. tit. 2. illat. 4. & princ. 2. & 4.*

68. *l. pen. §. 1. de in integ. rest. l. 1. de just. & jur. §. 1. Inst. de jur. nat. gent. & civili. Rom. c. 2. 14.15. 1. Cor. c. 5. 1.2. c. 11. 14. Siracid. c.17. 7. & seqq. Ezech. c. 5. 7.*

69. *1. Timoth. c. 2. 2. Rom. c. 2. 1. Corinth. c. 11. 14. c. 5. 1.2. Tit. c. 2. 12. Tob. c. 4.*

70. *Wesenb. in com. Inst. tit. de jur. nat. gent. & civili. & in com. D. eod. Connan. lib. 1. com. c. 4. Vacon. a Vacun. lib. 1. declar. c. 15. num. 3. vide Donell. lib. 1. com. c. 6.7. & Hotom. in §. 4. Instit. d. t. Govean. varior. c. 20.*

71. *d. l. 1. de just. & jur. §. 1. Instit. de jur. nat. gent. & civ. 1. Corinth. c. 11. 14. c. 5. 1.2. Rom. c. 2.*

72. *l. lex. 24. de stat. hom. l. 1. §. ult. de. furt. l. probrum. de verb. fig. §. quos. autem. Inst. de bon. possess. l. 34. §. 1. de contrah. empt. Cicer. lib. 1. offic.*

73. *l. 1. §. 1. si is qui test. liber. ess. juss. l. 1. de minor. d. §. 11. §. 39. thesauros. §. 40. per traditionem, Inst. de. rer. divis. l. 31. depos.*

74. *tit. Inst. de jure nat. gent. & civili. l. 1. de just. & jur. vide Connan. lib. 1. com. c. 6. Baron. in tit. Instit. de jur. natur. gent. Cujac. in l. 1. §. hujus de just. & jure.*

75. *§. 1. ibi, quod naturalis ratio. Inst. de jur. nat. gent. & civili. l. 9. de just. & jur.*

76. *l. 9. §. 2. l .pen. de just. & jur. §. 2 Instit. de jur. nat. gent. & civili. l. 25. l. 13. de legib. 1. Cor. c. 6. 3.4.*

77. *1. Thess. c. 4. 11.12. Rom. c. 12. 8. Eph. c. 6. 6. Eccles. c. 9. 10.*

78. *l. 1. de cont. empt. l. 1. de exerc. act. §. 2. Inst. de jur. nat. gent & civili. l. 51. §. 2. ubi Gothofr. ad L. Aquil. l. 5. de obl. & act. l. 17. §. 2. de instit. act. l. 21. com. divid. l. 1. §. 1. de his qui effuder. §. 10. item. Inst. de mandat. l. 1 de negot. gest.*

79. *§. 2. Instit. de jur. nat. gent. vide. Don. lib. 1. com. c. 7. Pinell. in rub. C. de rescind. vend. par. 1. nu. 11. & seqq.*

80. *arg. d. l. 9. §. 2. & d. §. 2. l. 25. l. 13. de legib. 1. Corinth. c. 6. 3.4.*

81. *§. 10 ubi Cujac. Inst. de. mand l. 70. ad Treb. l. 95. §. 7 de sol. l. 1. §. 1. 2. de his qui dejecer. effud. l. 8. §. 10. de minor. l. 32. §. 2. de adq. poss. l. 11. de praesc. verb. l. 44. §. eum qui de usucap. l. 1. de in integ. rest. l. 1. §. magistrum. de exerc. act. l. 1. naut. caup. stab. l. 8. depos.*

82. *§. 1. Inst. de oblig. quae quaes. ex cont. l. 5. de oblig. & act. l. 1. de neg. gest.*

83. *l. 41. de jur. dot. l. 82. de solut. l. 31. depos.*

84. *l. pen. de. just. & jur. l. 66. de condict. indeb. l. 6. §. 2. de jur. dot. l. 32. de reb. cred.*

85. *d. l. 31.*

86. *l. 4. de stat. hom. §. 1. Inst. de jure person. l. 4. de just. & jur. l. 1. de adq. rer. dom. §. singulorum 11. Inst. de rer. divis.*

87. *l. 3. l. 1. l. 7. §. 6. l. 9. §. 3. de adquir. rer. dom. §. 25. §. 39. §. 40. per traditionem. Instit. de rer. divis.*

88. Ed. note: Matthaeus Wesenbeck (1531–1586) was a legal scholar and professor at the University of Wittenberg.

89. *l. 5. de just. & jur.*

90. *vide Donell. lib. 1. com. cap. 7. Connan. lib. 1. com. c. 1. & 2. Huc pars magna tit. de just. & jure. & Instit. de jure nat. gent. & civili.*

Book 1, Chapter 14

On the Individual, Principal Law

In the previous chapter, I discussed common law; this chapter concerns individual law.

1. What Individual Law Is — Individual law is law that, having arisen from common law because of the benefit, necessity, or other circumstances of some particular state, is enacted by a magistrate. Or, it is law that, by the addition or subtraction of common law, a magistrate legally enacts and commands for the citizens of some particular location concerning future activities for the apparent benefit of the state.[1]

Individual law has groups and types.

2. Groups of Individual Law — It includes two groups: those in conformity with common law and those differing.[2]

3. Its Conformity with Natural Law — That is in conformity which does not depart entirely from common law, but is deduced in agreement with the same origin of each nature, from the embraced subject (namely to the business of the common law), and the just goal of both.[3]

4. Its Conformity with Natural Law — Because of this derivation of individual law from common law, individual law is accurately said to imitate common law.[4] Thus, common law is its guiding principle and pattern.[5] Because of this, common law is said to be unchangeable.[6]

5. Differences Between Them and Themselves — It differs when in its accommodation to a particular circumstance individual law sometimes departs from common law, that is, something is added or subtracted from it.[7] In other words, the difference occurs when some aspect of natural common law is not retained in every detail or when it does not remain in its general principles. Instead, while this law applies its nature and individual impact to specific situations and their circumstances, it is forced on some occasions to diverge quite a bit from common law in order to agree with the principle, embraced subject, and goal of common law.[8]

6. Differences Between Them and Themselves — Moreover, this individual law differs from common law, whenever common law is diminished or enhanced by it, for two very important reasons. In both instances, there is some necessity for adding or detracting from common law.[9]

7. Reasons for These Differences — One reason is the amount of information accessible to a lawgiver who, by his better and more convenient reason and method, applies common law to individual situations.[10] Or else it is the information accessible to someone who, by his degree of knowledge and understanding concerning the affairs and situations addressed, adds to or subtracts something from common law, as long as he returns or conforms this individual law to common law in agreement with, and consistent with, its origin, subject, and goal.[11] Now, because logical reasoning is the mother of this statute and law, and because this reasoning can grow in strength by its own offspring, therefore, changes necessarily occur.[12]

8. Reasons for These Differences — The other reason is the condition, nature, and state of the affair or of those things that are under the control and authority of the lawmaker, from which the individual law arises—namely, what kinds of individuals and situations are involved as well as what circumstances either precede or accompany them.[13] Because the condition and nature of all these things is various, diverse, inconsistent, and changeable, one cannot assert that the application of common law is one and the same in every matter and situation.[14]

9. Why This Law Is Changeable — For these two reasons, individual law is variable and changeable.[15] It is also said to be different from and unlike common law.[16] In fact, this simultaneous agreement and difference with common law is necessary. For, if it ordained the same thing as common law, it could not establish a type of law different from common law. If it wholly and in every way enacts something contrary to common law, it would not be law, and it would make common natural law changeable, which is impossible.

10. Examples of It — The prohibition of gifts between spouses provides one example of this individual law.[17] So does the prohibition of granting a loan to a son still under parental authority.[18] In both of these cases, there is no prohibition in common law.[19] Thus, it is possible for something to arise from common law by reason of its origin, subject, and aim that is said also to be in agreement with civil law.[20]

11. Types of Individual Law — There are two types of individual law: written and unwritten.[21] Some try to show that the act of writing is not essential to the essence of law.[22]

12. What Written Law Is — Civil law is written because it is enacted and promulgated in writing.[23] In fact, because all people do not have a capacity for it by nature, it is written down for fear that they would not be able to infer specific conclusions and laws from the general principles of common law for the nature and condition of their circumstances and every kind of activity, and for fear that they would not be able to remember it.

13. When It Takes Effect and Its Types — Written law receives its full strength within two months of the time of its promulgation,[24] unless it includes in itself a previous obligation or has come into public knowledge before its promulgation; or unless the knowledge of fraud along with the injury of another came together with the promulgating of the law; or unless it looks at previous events, or introduces exemptions, or was enacted with an invalid provision.[25]

Written law is principal or adjunct.[26]

14. Individual Principal Law and Its Names — Principal law is law that exists without adjunct law because it is contrasted with adjunct law, especially praetorian law.[27] Sometimes principal law is called expressive (ἐμφατικος).[28] It is variously understood that sometimes other laws arise from this law:[29] pure law,[30] formal law,[31] law simply and completely,[32] rigid law,[33] and established law.[34]

15. Types of Principal Law — Principal law has two parts—that is, law that is established by the whole population or by a portion of the population[35]—and it is distributed in different places because it is enacted either by consent, as in the case of a statute or popular decree, or by exigent circumstances, as in the case of a decision of the senate.[36]

16. What a Statute (*lex*) Is — A statute is a law established by the whole Roman people that they enacted in their popular assemblies when a senatorial magistrate made a formal request as consul, and after the votes of the people in their assemblies had been counted.[37] In other authors, the term *lex* is understood differently.[38]

A law is enacted by a portion of the Roman population, as necessity advises,[39] either by many or by one.[40]

If it is established by many, it is a popular decree or a decision of the senate.

17. What a Popular Decree Is — A popular decree is a law that the plebian class of the Roman people in their tribal assemblies established by their own vote when a plebian magistrate, such as the plebian tribune (δήμαρχος), made a formal request in the capacity of their leader.[41] This law later obligated the whole population by the Hortensian law[42] and was called a statute.[43]

18. What a Decision of the Senate Is — A decision of the senate is a law that the senate ordered and established by its own vote through division or the decision of a majority.[44] Later, it included decisions made by the intervention of the emperor.[45] The *Juris Civilis* declares that this law has an established necessity.[46]

19. Law Enacted by an Emperor and Its Name — Principal and pure civil law established by one person[47] is that which an emperor, after being advised by his prefects,[48] established and answered in writing by imperial rescript, or by answering a supplicant's petition.[49] It also includes those letters that the appointed quaestors of magistrates would read;[50] what the emperor ordered to be signed in his own name;[51] what he decreed after recognizing a problem;[52] anticipated in an edict;[53] or established by applying and consulting the sources of the *Juris Civilis*;[54] or in a speech given in the senate regarding a law about to be enacted, with the senate deciding after hearing.[55] For this reason, it is called an imperial decision published in legal inquiries,[56] a mandate, an imperial constitution,[57] a rescript, a decree, an edict, a constitution, an imperial enactment,[58] a religious rescript,[59] an imperial declaration,[60] a divine sanction,[61] a most holy constitution, an order, a most holy statute,[62] and others. A decision of the senate is a law that is established when the judgment and advice of the senate is employed.[63]

Should any uncertainty have appeared concerning this law, the emperor was called.[64] Very often this type of law is separated from the other types of civil law.[65] It is similar to a statute.[66] A decree is properly said to be established when it is made within the limits of an individual or other circumstances.[67] An edict is a law that has been established when these things are missing.[68]

20. Suffrage and Duties of the Elders During the Time of the Jews — Concerning the voting of elders in the time of the Jews, see 2 Samuel 5:3; Judges 20; Luke 22:66; Numbers 11:16; Deuteronomy 21:2, 19, 20; 13:5; 1 Kings 7;[69] 2 Chronicles 1; Joshua 23; Matthew 15:2; 16:21; and 26:3, 47, 57. For examples of imperial edicts, see Luke 2:1; Daniel 2:12; 3:5; 6:9, 26; Genesis 12:20; Exodus 1:15, 16; 1 Kings 12:26, 27, 28; 2 Chronicles 15:17;[70] and Esther 1:19; 3:13, 15; 8:13. Wise elders even used to assist kings in lawmaking: 1 Chronicles 13:1, 2; 38:1, 2; 2 Chronicles 20:20; Numbers 30:1; Deuteronomy 5:29, 30; 29:1; 1 Chronicles 28:1, 2; 2 Chronicles 5:2, 3; Psalm 121;[71] Isaiah 3:15, 16;[72] Joshua 9:15; Jeremiah 36:14ff.; 37:14ff.[73]

Notes

1. *l. 1. l. 2. de constit. princ. §. lex. & seqq. Instit. de jure nat. gent. & civil. l. 6. de just. & jur. l. 13. l. 16. l. 25. de legib. vide Johan. Rosin. lib. 8. antiquit. c. 2. 3 & lib. 6. c. 9. 10.11. Menoch. lib. 2. arb. cas. 185. Connan. lib. 1. com. cap. 9.*
2. *arg. l. 6. de just. & jure.*
3. *d. l. 6. l. 9. de justit. & jure. l. 2. ex quibus caus. maior. Calvin. lib. 4. Instit. c. 20. sect. 16. Junius de politia Mos. observat.*
4. *l. 1. ibi naturalem aequitatem secutus de minorib. l. 1. de pact. l. 1. de constit. pecun. l. 7. de in integr. rest. §. minorem. 4. Inst. de adopt. Zanchius de legib. human. thes. 6. c. 10. de redempt. opera. Petr. Martyr. Gen. c. 2.2.*
5. *Franc. Jun. de polit. Mos. observ. Zanch. d. c. 10. thes. 1. de lege natura.*
6. *§. pen. Inst. de jur. nat. gent. & civil. l. pen de just. & jure. Zanchius d. locis.*
7. *l. 6. de just. & jur. l. 16. de legib.*
8. *Jun. & Zanch d. locis. Dd. in l. 6. de just. & jur.*
9. *d. l. 6. de just. & jur. l. 2. de const. princ. Calvin. lib. 4. Inst. c. 20. sect. 16.*
10. *l. 26. l. 27 & seqq. de legib. Franc. Jun. de polit. Mos. observat.*
11. *d. l. 6. & l. 7. de in integr. rest. l. 1. ex quib. caus. major. l. 1. ad SC. Macedon. l. 1. de donas. inter vir. & uxor.*

12. *Jun. & Zanch. d. loc.*
13. *l. 16. de poen. §. fin. Instit. de jure nat. gent.*
14. *l. 11. l. 16 de poen. l. 8. de transact. l. 2. 3. 4. ubi pupill. educar.*
15. *§. pen. Institut. de jur. nat. gent. & civili. l. 26. & seqq. de legibus.*
16. *l. 16. de legib. §. 2. Instit. de jure nat. gent. & civil. §. pen. d. t.*
17. *tit. de donat. inter vir. & uxor.*
18. *l. 1. & tit. tot. ad SC. Macedon.*
19. *l. in re. C. mandat.*
20. *§. 1. Inst. de tutel. §. pen. Inst. de Attil. tut. tit. Instit. de pat. potest. §. 4. Instit. de adopt.*
21. *§. 3. Institut. de jur. nat. gent. & civil. l. 32. l. 33. de legib.*
22. *ex l. 6. de justit. & jure. l. 2. §. ex his. de orig. jur. l. 32. & seqq. de legibus. vide Connan. lib. 1. com. cap. 7. num. 5. Donell. libr. 1. com. c. 13. Wesenb. in com. tit. de legib. Anton. Fab. Jurisprud. tit. 2. princip. 6.*
23. *l. 10. l. 36. ubi Bartol. de legib. l. 8. C. d. t. Baro in §. lex. Inst. de just. & jur. Guid. Pap. decis. 91. num. Donell. libr. 1. com. cap. 13. Connan. d. loc. c. 8. adde Deut. cap. 31. 25.26. cap. 17. 19. Josu. 8. 32. 2. Chron. cap. 33. 16. cap. 34. 8.33. cap. ult. 22.23. 1. Esdr. cap. 1. 1.2. cap. 6. 11. cap. 7. 13.21. Esther. 1. 19. Psalm. 149. 9.10. ubi Jun. per Deut. cap. 12. 32. cap. 29. cap. 4. 6. & seqq.*
24. *Novell. 66. vide Menoch. libr. 2. arb. cas. 185. Gabriel. tit. de legib. concl. 4. lib. 6. Duaren. tit. de justit. & jure c. 2. c. 4. Connan. lib. 1. com. c. 9. num. 8.*
25. *Menoch. d. cas. 185. Gabriel. d. conclus. 4. & 3.*
26. Ed. note: Althusius discusses adjunct (or accessory) law in the following chapter of the *Dicaeologicae*, which is not included in this translation.
27. *§. 1. tit. Inst. de oblig. l. 1. quib. mod. ususfr. amitt. l. 9. §. 1. usuf. quemad. cav. l. 1. §. ult. l. 3. §. 12. de constit. pecun. §. sed ista. Inst.*

de action. l. scio. 14. de testib. l. 20. §. 7. qui test. fac. poss. l. 27. de reg. jur. §. 1. Inst. de perpet. & temp. act. l. 1. de pact. Donell. in §. sed ista. & in §. actiones. num. 7. Instit. de act.

28. *l. 1. §. fin. de superfic. l. 1. §. 5. quod fals. tut. l. 1. quib. mod. ususfr. amitt. l. 9. §. 1. usufr. quemad. cav. §. actiones 10. §. sed ista. Instit. de act. l. 27. de reg. jur. §. 2. Instit. de bon. poss. l. 8. de reb. eor. qui sub tutel. l. 1. de curat. fur. l. 27. §. 2. de pact. l. 4. de compens. late. Brisson. lib. 9. de verb. sign. & lib. 3. de solut. Cujac. ad Paul. lib. 3. sent. tit. 6. §. 17. & ad Ulpian. tit. 26.*

29. *vid. Tiraquell. in l. si unquam verb. revertatur 20. & seqq. C. de revoc. donat.*

30. *l. 4. §. 27. ubi Cujac. de usucap. l. 32. in fine. d. tit. l. 16. de minor. l. 36. de admin. tut. Cujac. libr. 8. obs. c. 16.*

31. *l. 27. de reg. jur.*

32. *l. 1. quib. mod. ususfr. amitt. l. 9. §. 1. usufr. quem. cav. l. 60. de fidejuss.*

33. *l. pen. 30. de constit. pecun. vide Duar. in l. 5. nu. 14. de in lit. jurand.*

34. *l. 27. de pact. l. Nesennius 34. de negot. gest. 1. 6. de in integr. rest. l. adultery. ad L. Jul. de adult. l. in heredem. de calum. l. 48. in sine de jure. fisci. Brisson. lib. 3. de solut. tit. 1. & lib. 9. de verb. signif. in voce. jus & Fab. 1. jurispr. passim.*

35. *l. 2. §. 10. 11. §. 9. de origin. jur. l. 32. §. 1. de legib.*

36. *l. pen. de legib. §. senatusconsultum. Inst. de jur. nat. gent. & civ. l. 2 de orig. jur. Cujac. libr. 14. obs. c. 16. Gell. lib. 10. cap. 10. Alexand. ab Alexand. lib. 6. gen. dier. c. 23.*

37. *vid. Johan. Rosin. in antiq. Roman. lib. 8. cap. 2. 3. & lib. 6. c. 9. 10. 14. arg. §. 4. Inst. de jure natur. gent. & civili. ubi Theophil. l. 1. fam. hercisc.*

38. *tit. de legib. l. 9. C. de donat. tit. de L. Commissor.*

39. *l. 2. §. 10. 11. de orig. jur.*

40. *l. 2. §. 11. de orig. jur.*

41. *§. 4. Instit. de jure nat. gent. & civ. l. 1 ad L. Aquil. l. 2. §. 8. 9. de origin. jur. l. 238. de verborum signif. adde 1. Sam. c. 8. Judic. c. 11. Johan. c. 9. 15. & seqq. 2. Macchab. c. 10. 8.*

42. *l. 2. §. 8. de orig jur. Contius lib. 2. c. 18. subsecivar. Alex. ab Alex. lib. 15. c. 26.*

43. *l. 1 ad l. Aquil. l. 1. ad L. Falcid. d. l. 2. §. 8.*

44. *l. 9. de legib. §. 5. Instit. de jur. nat. gent. & civil. l. 2. ad SC. Vellej. tit. Instit. de SC. Tertyl. tit. de SC. Orphit. tit. ad SC. Trebell. Rosin. libr. 7. cap. 7. antiq. Rom. Cujac. lib. 14. observ. c. 16.*

45. *l. 1. de reb. eor. qui sub tutel. Duaren. de just. & jur. cap. 3. Alex. ab Alexand. libr. 4. cap. 11. gen. dier. Gell. libr. 4. cap. 7.*

46. *l. pen. de legib. l. 2. §. 9. ubi Cujac. de origin. jur.*

47. *l. 2. §. 11. de orig. jur.*

48. *§. 2. Instit. de his qui sunt sui, vel alien. jur.*

49. *l. 1. de const. princ. l. 3. §. Divus. de sepul. viol. l. 13. de reb. eor. l. ult. in fine. de offic. procur. Casar. l. 31. §. 14. de recept. arb. l. 5. de magist. conven. Esth. c. 8. 8. & seqq. Daniel. c. 6. 15.*

50. *l. 1. in fin. de. off. quaest.*

51. *l. rescriptum. de distract. pign. vid. epigraphen l. 1. de offic. praef. praetor. Brisson. lib. 3. selectar. c. 7.*

52. *l. pen. de his quae in testam. del. d. l. 31. §. 14.*

53. *§. 6. Instit. de jur. nat. gent. & civil. ubi Theophil. tit. de constit. princip. Duaren. lib. 2. disp. c. 19. Govean libr. 2. var. c. 30.*

54. *in princ. Instit. de codicill. l. 33. in fine de admin. tut. tit. de constit. princip. in epigraphe l. 20. de rit. nupt.*

55. *l. 1. l. 2. de feriis. l. 2. de serv. fugit. l. cum his. de donat. inter vir. & uxor. l. 1. §. 1. ne de stat. defunct. l. 1. de reb. eor. qui sub. l. item veniunt. §. praeter. l. illud. l. si & rem. de petit. hered. l. 1. C. d. t.*

l. 8. de transact. l. 2. C. de curat. fur. l. 9. ad SC. Tertyll. l. 16. de sponsal. Brisson. lib. 1. c. 16 select.

56. *vide l. ult. ad SC Trebell. epigraphen l. 11. de jure patron. l. 81. ubi Gothofred. ad SC. Trebell. Cujac. lib. 2. obs. c. 28.*

57. *tit. C. de mandat. princ. l. 3. l. 19. de offic. praesid. §. 6. Instit. de jur. nat. gent.*

58. *l. 11. de legib. tit. de constit. princ. l. 33. de adm. tut. l. 19. §. pen. locat. l. pen. §. 1. de jure patron. tit. C. de divers. rescript. & pragm. sanct. l. 1. ex quib. caus. major. l. ult. C. de prox. sacri scrin.*

59. *l. 1. Cod. de monopol.*

60. *§. illud 11. Inst. de adopt. l. pen. C. de. haret. & Manich. l. 11. C. de vect. & commiss.*

61. *l. ult. C. de. hared. & Manich.*

62. *l. 7. C. de pagan. l. 5. §. 5 de adm. tut. l. leges. C. de legib.*

63. *l. 8. de transact. l. eleganter. §. 1 de condict. indeb.*

64. *l. 97. de leg. 3. l. ult. de jur. fisc. l. 16. de rit. nupt. l. 20. §. item. de petit. hered. l. 1. l. 2. de fer. Cujac. in l. 8. de transact.*

65. *l. 4. §. contra. de dol. mal & met. except. l. 33. de cond. & demonst. Cujac. lib. 7. obs. c. 19.*

66. *§. 2. Inst. de bon. poss. l. 8. de legib. §. sed & quod. Inst. de jur. nat. gent. vid. l. 8. C. de legib.*

67. *Cujac. in parat. C. de divers. rescript. & prag. sanct.*

68. *l. 8. de quaestio. l. 13. de jure fisci. Theophil. in §. sed & quod. Instit. de jure nat. gent. & civili.*

69. Ed. note: This citation should probably refer to 1 Kings 8.

70. Ed. note: This citation probably contains an error.

71. Ed. note: Psalm 122 in many modern versions. Here Althusius appears to be following the Vulgate numbering of the Psalms.

72. Ed. note: Isaiah 3:14 and 15 in the common versification. Here Althusius is following the versification in the late sixteenth-century Latin translation of the Bible by Immanuel Tremellius and Franciscus Junius.

73. *Hujus loci est titulus de just. & jur. tit. de orig. jur. tit. de legib. tit. de constit. princ. tit. Cod. de divers. rescript. & pragm. sanct. tit. C. de legib. C. de mandat. princ.*

Book 1, Chapter 32

On Public Power in General

I have discussed private power and its domain. Now I will turn to public power.[1]

1. What Public Power Is — Public power is what has been granted to someone from the body of an association,[2] with a territory, for the purpose of caring for and administering the business, affairs, and individuals of the associated body.[3]

2. What Its Territory Is — Territory, in general, is the place or all the plots of land within a city's limits inside which this power and authority is exercised.[4] This is called a diocese or district.[5]

This public power is universal, noble, and highest, or limited and specific.

3. Public Power in General — Highest or universal power is that which is granted to someone by a universal association[6] with a territory belonging to a universal kingdom[7] so that in accordance with the regulations of the Ten Commandments[8] and royal authority[9] this person may administer the laws and affairs of the associated body for its own benefit[10] and so that he may care for them and oversee their administration.[11]

4. Its Various Titles — It is called the highest of things, holy command, excellent law,[12] majesty,[13] absolute power,[14] eminence,[15] lordship over the populace,[16] the highest command,[17] and the burden.[18] In addition, subjects who submit to lesser magistrates, as well as higher magistrates who submit to guardians, are also included.[19]

5. Laws and Affairs of a Kingdom — The laws and affairs of a kingdom, state, or universal association are those that are established as common to each and every one of its members for its benefit and out of necessity. For this reason, whatever things are by ownership part of the universal association, by administration controlled by the state body, and by duty under the highest magistrate,[20] are called regalia.

This universal administration of the highest magistrate is under public business or public things.

The general and universal administration of the public business of a state is either ecclesiastic or civil.

6. What Ecclesiastic Administration Is — The ecclesiastic administration is that which manages ecclesiastic public business—namely, whatever pertains to the first table of the Decalogue. That is, the worship, the doctrine of the pure and orthodox faith, and public profession are introduced and established, and the exercise and freest enjoyment of them by anyone who wishes, according to the command of the Word of God, is allowed, defended, protected, and transmitted to later generations.[21]

7. What Civil Administration Is — The civil or secular administration is that which manages public business—namely, whatever pertains to the enjoyment of this life (and, hence, is secular), and to the second table of the Decalogue. This administration is overseen by a magistrate for the benefit of the subjects and the well-being of the state.[22]

This civil administration looks partly to preserving the external conduct in a common society and partly to the advantage of the life of the society.

8. The Subjects of the Administration Concerning External Discipline — The following powers look to preserving external conduct: (1) the power to pass legislation, (2) the power to punish, (3) the power to maintain public safety, and (4) the power to declare and wage war and to establish peace.[23]

9. The Subjects of the Administration Concerning the Common Good — Administration pertaining to the common good of the society is that by which the social life of the citizens and members living in the state is promoted and protected. This administration consists of the following: (1) the oversight of commerce, (2) the oversight of coinage, (3) the oversight of language, (4) the distribution of duties and responsibilities, (5) the granting of exceptions and immunities, (6) agreements, and (7) final appeals. Each of these things will look after good order (εὐνομία), good conduct (εὐταχία), and self-sufficiency (αὐτάρκεια).[24]

10. What the Administration of Public Things Is — The administration of public things is that by which the highest magistrate administers the things pertaining to the state according to its well-being, just like a guardian or a caretaker to whom a magistrate is often compared.[25]

11. What the Goods of the State Are — Things pertaining to a universal association or a state are goods that have been set apart for its use.[26] If these goods are immovable, they are called the patrimony of the crown, kingdom, or state.[27]

12. The Types of These Goods — Things of this sort include tribute, contributions, rent, land-use taxes, public possessions, fines, confiscated property, unclaimed inheritances, weapons, public records, the treasury, fields, estates, revenues, villages, towns, cities, regions, the imperial court, duchys, marquessates, episcopates, baronies, and castles.[28] They also include royal roads, public roads, docks, defenses, and many other such things.[29]

13. The Administration of These Things — The administration of public things is conducted for the benefit of the state when those things are employed and expended by the highest magistrate for the discharge of his duties and for the necessary and beneficial uses of the state.

14. The Purpose of Public Disbursements and Expenditures — For this reason, the necessity of disbursing and expending public things is twofold. First, it provides support for the highest magistrate. Second, it maintains the administration of public business because it looks to the cost and expense by which the profits of the state are advanced and its losses and expenditures are diverted and impeded.[30] If anything remains in the state's treasury it must be stored and preserved for whatever future necessity may come.[31]

15. Public Administration When It Looks at Private Affairs — There is also a type of public administration that looks to the affairs and the character of private citizens and subjects, by which the highest magistrate by his care, foresight, and governance maintains and defends the persons and goods of his subjects against violence and injury, and he guides and governs in order to direct the symbiotic political livelihood of the state by avoiding its harm and promoting its welfare.

16. What the Goods of Subjects Are — The things and goods of subjects are (1) life and bodily safety, (2) reputation and good name, and (3) external moveable and immoveable goods.

Against these goods various plots are constructed and injuries are inflicted that the magistrate ought to remove in every way, to the extent that he is able, as if he were the subjects' guardian or defender. In the first place, he will punish and remove those vagabonds, sorcerers, beggars, thugs, dice-players, game-players, actors, mimes, comedians, pimps, loan sharks, hucksters, and originators of other evils and harmful desires who swindle and rob the subjects in unlawful ways and who deprive them of their possessions and do damage to their reputations and good character. He will also remove bandits, highwaymen, muggers, thieves, and looters, who harm the bodies, lives, or possessions of the subjects. He will set up guardians for wasters and spendthrifts. He will provide for future fires and floods. Finally, he will take care of and provide for whatever else magistrates do for the defense and protection of the goods of their subjects.[32]

17. In What Things the Public Concern of Persons and Subjects Is — He will have responsibility over the care of individuals so that they might be educated and instructed in public schools or workshops for the well-being of the state and so that no one is unemployed, so that the harmony of different segments of society and different members of the state is maintained, so that the administration of justice might be weighty and sincere, so that evil habits and extravagance might be removed and restrained, and so that crimes might be punished.[33]

18. The Care of the Poor — Most importantly, he will have responsibility over the care of those who need pity, such as the blind, the mute, the deaf, the mad, the orphans, the old, the poor, the leprous, and the like for whose survival he will establish a yearly income, public houses for the reception of strangers, clinics, hospitals, orphanages, poorhouses, and nursing homes.[34]

19. The Care of Good Government and the Types of Public Power — Finally, he will make provisions so that his subjects are not burdened and impoverished by tyranny, excessive taxation, and servitude.[35]

Next, concerning the types of this public power, there are two: monarchic power and polyarchic power.

20. What Monarchic Power Is — Monarchic power is that which is granted to one person. This power must be strengthened by the help of good citizens so that the state, divided by the authority of many, might not be torn to pieces. Furthermore, public assemblies must be strengthened in their authority so that a monarchy's legal power might not be transformed into tyranny.[36]

Polyarchic power is the alternation of administration among many people, which is equal to a shared authority. In turn, its types are aristocratic and democratic.

21. What Aristocratic Power Is — Aristocratic power is the highest public power and is granted jointly and indivisibly to a few colleagues. So that an aristocracy might not degenerate into a monarchy or a democracy, it must be strengthened by special legislation.

22. What Democratic Power Is — Democratic power is that which is granted to certain individuals out of the population by exchange, turn, or succession, at certain times, and who are chosen by a universal body of fellow citizens for a particular circumstance so that by assembly, company, or tribe, they might administer the state. So that a democracy might not degenerate into a monarchy or an aristocracy, it must be strengthened by certain special legislation.[37]

Notes

1. *vide sup. c. 27. n. 4.*

2. *Covarru. pract. quaest. c. 1. n. 2. 3. 4. c. 4. 3. Vasquius illust. quaest. lib. 1. c. 8. c. 18. c. 1. c. 2. Deut. c. 17. 14. & seqq. Judic. c. 8. 2.23. c. 9. 6. c. 11. 2.10. & seqq. 1. Sam. c. 8. l. 1. de constitut. princip. l. 2. §. 33. de orig. jur.*

3. *arg. l. 13. l. 19. l. 6. l. 9. l. 11. 12. de offic. praesidis. Rom. c. 13. 4. & seqq. Exod. c. 18. 17.22. Deut. c. 1. 4.12. Num. c. 11. 17.18. l. 2. §. 33. de orig. jur. Novell. 60. cap. 2 & Novell. 85. vide quae diximus in Polit. cap. 18. & seqq.*

4. *l. 239. §. pupillus §. territorium. de verb. sign. l. ult. de jurisd.*

5. *Hieron. de monte, finium reg. c. 7. c. 12.*

6. *hanc potestatem & jus constituendi atque ordinandi habere Remp. testatur Vasquius lib. 1. c. 47. cont. illustr. Bart. & alii in l. omnes. de justit. & jur. diximus Polit. c. 9. c. 18. Ratione proprietatis & dominii, hec potestas est penes Remp. Molynaus in consuetud. Parisiens. tit. 1. §. 1. gloss. 7. n. 9. Peregrinus lib. 1. §. hactenus. n. 71. 74. de jure fisci. Paurmeist. de jurisd. lib. 1. c. 1. num. 19. & 42. Vasquius lib. 1. in praefat. illust. Covarruv. pract. quaest. c. 4. vid. Polit. c. 19. ubi diximus.*

7. *de hoc universali territorio, sub se alia particularia territoria regionum distinctarum complectente, vide Decian. consil. 123. n. 17. & seqq. vol. 3. Andr. Knichen de sublimi & regio territorio, per tot. Zas. consil. 16. n. 46. vol. 2. Matth. Stephani de jurisd. lib. 2. part. 1. c. 7. num. 3. 4. 5.*

8. *Deut. cap. 17. 20.21. Josu. c. 1. 8. 1. Sam. c. 10. 25. 2. Reg. c. 11. 12. c. 23. 2.3. Daniel. cap. 6. 9.16. Esth. c. 8. 8. l. digna vox. C. de legib. Novell. 105. c. 2. l. filius 15. de cond. instit. vide quae diximus in Polit. c. 18. c. 21. c. 24.*

9. *Deut. cap. 17. 15.16. in Polit. c. 19 diximus.*

10. *Ezech. c. 34. Jerem. c. 22. 3. & seqq. Psalm. 82. 1.2.3.4. & 72. 1.2. & seqq. Novell. 85. late diximus in Polit. c. 18. c. 19. c. 24. Absolutam igitur & plenissimam potestatem princeps non habet, Covarruv. lib. 3. var. resol. c. 6. n. 8. Pinell. in l. 2. c. 2. rub. C. de rescind. vend. Vasq. lib. 1. illust. quaest. cap. 26. num. 22. Pruckman. de regalib. §. soluta potestas. c. 3. Faber jurisprud. tit. 2. confut. 2. & illat. 2. diximus late lib. Polit. c. 18. 19. c. 24.*

11. *diximus in Polit. c. 1. quid sit regere, dirigere, gubernate, vel imperare.*

12. *Clapmar. de arcan. Rerumpub. lib. 1. c. 10. Bornicius de majest. politica cap. 13.*

13. *tit. ad L. Jul. majest. late de hoc vocabulo Bornicius d. loc. c. 1. & plerique lexicographi.*

14. *l. 1. de const. princip. Luc. c. 4. 6. Johan. c. 19. 11. Roman. c. 13. 1.2.3.*

15. *1. Timoth. c. 2. 2. Juda cap. 1. 8.*

16. *Judic. cap. 5. 13. cap. 8. 22. 23. & 9. 2. cap. 15. 11. c. 14. 5. 1. Chron. c. 4. 22. Psalm. 105. 20.21 & 106. 41. Esa. c. 3. 13.*

17. *d. l. 1. l. 2. §. 14. 15. & seqq. de orig. jur. l. 23. de injur. l. 7. §. 1. de capt. & post lim. revers. Coloss. c. 1. 16. c. 2. 10. Ephes. c. 5. 21. & seqq.*

18. *Exod. cap. 18. 18.23. Deut. cap. 1. 12.13. 1. Reg. cap. 9. 19. Num. cap. 11. 16.17.18.*

19. *Zoannet. de Imp. Roman. num. 178. & seqq. diximus in Polit. c. 18. De publica potestate JC. Julium. libros. conscripsisse, patet ex epigraph. l. 1. de offic. quaestor.*

20. *Covarru. pract. quaest. cap. 1. num. 2. 3. 4. c. 4. num. 3. l. 1. de constit. princ. diximus. cap. 19. in Polit. Deut. c. 17. 14.15. & seqq.*

21. *De hac prolixe diximus cap. 9. & c. 28. Politicor.*

22. *Roman. cap. 13. 1. Pet. cap. 2. 1. Sam. cap. 12. 5.6. de quae prolixe in cap. 10. & seqq. & c. 29. & seqq. Politicorum diximus.*

23. *de quibus abunde in Politicis diximus. & Rosenthal libr. 1. cap. 5. de feud. Dd. in cap. unic. quae sunt regal.*

24. *vide infra c. 81. de quibus singulis in Politicis diffuse egimus. & Dd. in c. unico. quae sunt regalia.*

25. *diximus in Polit. c. 18. & cap. 37.*

26. *Ezech. cap. 45. & 46. Choppinus lib. 1. tit. 1. de doman. regis. arg. l. 3. §. ult. de jur. fisci. l. cum servus. §. constat. de legat. 1.*

27. *Choppin. d. loco. vid. supra c. 21. n. 29. & seqq.*

28. *Choppin. lib. 1. tit. 2. & 5. de doman. reg.*

29. *in Polit. cap. 17. & cap. 37. diximus, & supra cap. 21.*

30. *vid. cap. 27. Politic.*

31. *d. cap. 27.*

32. *diximus d. cap. 37.*

33. *l. 13. de offic. praesid.*

34. *dixi in Polit. cap. 37.*

35. *vid. c. 38. Politic.*

36. *Osor. lib. 8. de reg. Instit.*

37. *de quibus singulis diximus in Politic. cap. 39. De materia hujus capitis vivendi Dd. in c. unic. quae sunt regal tit. de constit. princip. tit. ad L. Jul. majest. tit. de adminst. rer. ad civit. pertin.*

Book 1, Chapter 33

On Limited Public Power

I have already spoken about highest or universal public power. Now I will turn to limited or special public power.

1. What Limited Public Power Is — Limited, special, or inferior public power is that which is legally rendered for a particular, limited, and restricted territory and is undertaken on behalf of the highest power that it recognizes as its superior and to whom it is held accountable for its administration.[1]

This limited public power, in turn, is either provincial or official.

2. What Provincial Power Is — Provincial power is that which the governor of a province exercises in the territory of his own province with his own legal authority.

3. What a Province Is — A province is something that in the scope of its own territory contains many villages, towns, castles, or cities being associated and closely united within the community and administration of one legal authority. It is also called a region or a district.[2] Today, any city having a distinct and separate government and territory is called a province.[3]

4. The Authority of a Provincial Governor in the Past and Present — Formerly the governor of a province would administer and rule one or more provinces,[4] and his power and office were temporary. However, at the time of Charlemagne these governorships became perpetual and hereditary, and the jurisdiction of them was inherited.[5] Today, these governorships in the German states are of two types: some are directly subject to the Empire, like states are; others are indirectly subject to the Empire.[6]

5. What a Governor of Many Provinces Is Today — A governor of many provinces is called a prince, a duke, a marquis, or a landgrave.[7]

6. What Power a Provincial Governor Has — The governor of a province enjoys full jurisdiction and power within the territory of his own province in which he also presides over what are called the regalia.[8]

7. What Power Is Reserved for the Highest Magistrate — The provincial governor enjoys this power with the exception of the following, which are reserved for the highest magistrate:

1. Seniority, preeminence, and universal jurisdiction in each and every province of the kingdom.[9]
2. The promulgation of universal legislation effective through the entire kingdom and each individual province.
3. The right to summon assemblies and councils.
4. The right to declare war and peace.
5. The right to found universal studies and academies.
6. The right to appoint princes, dukes, marquis, counts, barons, nobles, notaries, and the right to deprive one of such a title.
7. The right to assign rent on public land.
8. The right to grant traditional annual market days.
9. The right to set up a postal service.

10. The right to grant citizenship.
11. The right to legitimize and restore parentage.
12. The right to restore reputation and honor.
13. The right to set the age of majority.
14. The right to grant immunities and privileges.
15. The right of public safety.
16. The right to coin money.
17. The right of final appeal and diverting court cases.
18. The right to judge the disputes of dukes, counts, and other dignitaries.
19. The right of universal ban and proscription.

Each and every one of these powers is reserved for the highest magistrate and cannot be shared or passed down to a provincial power. They cannot be usurped or exercised by them.[10] To this list I add the right to inspect and to coerce, which the highest magistrate exercises over the governor of a province.[11]

8. What Jurisdiction a Provincial Governor Has — The governor of this sort of province has the use-right of jurisdiction and command, their personal use and full exercise, with a certain free administration.[12] Although he cannot yield this use-right to another, and he cannot resign himself from it,[13] nevertheless, as long as the power to recall this right is maintained,[14] he can impose the exercise of this command onto another person.[15] He does not, however, have lasting and full ownership of this jurisdiction. Therefore, when the use-right of this power comes to an end, it is returned to the highest magistrate who gave it and is consolidated with his retained command.[16] For this reason, it is often said that all jurisdictions flow from the highest magistrate and flow back to him.

9. What Limited Command (*imperium*) Is — The exercise of this power and command is appropriate when it is in accordance with the will and direction of the highest magistrate,[17] when it falls within the mandate that has granted this power,[18] and when the accountability of its administration to the highest magistrate is guaranteed.[19]

10. What Official Power Is — Official public power is that which is granted to someone without territorial rights in order to perform those things that must be done for the accounting of public office.[20]

Official public power is twofold: true public power or public power with some limit.

11. What Official Public Power Is — True official public power is that which is granted by reason of a political office or magistracy with jurisdiction or its own command[21] in a foreign territory onto an individual and his cases and business,[22] and it is literally called a magistracy.[23]

12. What Command and Its Types Are — Command is the power to investigate, enact, order, and punish;[24] it is also called jurisdiction.[25]

This command is either mixed or pure[26] and of a good breadth (εὐπλατής), and each is called jurisdiction.[27]

13. What Mixed Command Is — Mixed command is the power a magistrate has to investigate what has happened in some affair and to institute policy in that case according to what is right and deserved and according to the prescribed limit and right of the magistracy that he possesses.[28]

14. Its Titles and Members — In other places it is called not pure command[29] but power inborn, innate, or interwoven with the magistracy, or something similar.[30] For this reason, it began to be called mixed because it is not only bare and separate, as pure command is, but it is also mixed with or joined to a magistracy, office, or service by a public injunction.[31]

Mixed command has two parts: the power of inquiry and the power of establishment.

15. What the Power of Judicial Inquiry Is — The power of inquiry is the judicial examination or investigation of some affair.[32] Even though judicial examination is often confused with jurisdiction,[33] this inquiry revolves most of all around the nature of an action so that it might learn for itself a full representation and arrangement with all the attending circumstances, by which it might be able to establish the legality of an action.[34] Therefore, there is a formal trial and a judicial representative.[35] Some call this simple jurisdiction.[36]

16. What the Power of Establishment (*statuendi*) Is — The power of establishment is that which makes a determination concerning a law and applies it to an investigated action with the carrying out of a decreed law or by executive power.[37] A decreed law depends on a command; the execution of a decreed law is carried out through moderate coercion.[38]

17. What an Order Is — An order, therefore, arises from the power of establishment, ordering, and commanding.[39] Included with it is the right to prohibit.[40]

18. Its Specific Title — In other places, it is listed, in kind, as jurisdiction, that is, as the right to settle, determine, and enact law.[41] Because of this, an edict of a praetor, in which he orders or prohibits, is often called jurisdiction.[42] Granted, order is said to pertain more to command.[43]

19. The Right to Defend Against Injury — The power to order and to prohibit also includes the right to defend oneself from violence and injury.[44] It also includes the power to ordain and establish anything that pertains to the safety of the subjects.[45]

20. What Moderate Coercion Is — Moderate coercion comes from the power of establishing law and carrying out decrees by applying force or assessing fines[46] or by announcing or inflicting any punishment not capital.[47] This is called moderate coercion, with respect to pure command,[48] or it is called greater command in the same jurisdiction with respect to an order.[49] By no means does the fact that it is greater command make it absolute command.[50]

21. Arbitrary Moderate Coercion and the Types of Mixed Command — Moderate coercion, which ought to be assessed in accordance with the logic of the circumstances, is left to the decision of a judge.[51]

There are two types of mixed command: first, that for which jurisdiction is included; second, that for which jurisdiction is added.[52]

22. Under Whose Jurisdiction Mixed Command Is — Mixed command to which jurisdiction has been included and intermixed by its own nature occurs when the right or use of command is exercised primarily in the situation.[53] In other words, it is that command in which the power and authority of command stands out more than that of jurisdiction.[54] Matthias Stephani[55] incorrectly rejects this type.

23. How Mixed Command Includes Jurisdiction — Mixed command for which jurisdiction is added is the term for command that is exercised not primarily for its own sake but in order to exhibit jurisdiction or because of an order.[56] With this limitation, jurisdiction or order eludes some situations and lacks an outlet.[57] Therefore, in this case, jurisdiction prevails.[58]

24. Sole Jurisdiction Never Exists — From these ideas, it is the case that jurisdiction is never alone, but either it is attached to command or is a part of it.[59] Because of this inseparable association, it is rightly said that whatever things are attributed to jurisdiction are also rightly attributed to command[60] so that command may be called jurisdiction and vice versa.[61]

25. Why It Is Called Mixed Command — Thus, from here it is also inferred why it is called mixed command—that is, because it is tied to jurisdiction.[62]

26. What Pure Command Is — Pure command is what is given not by the right of a magistrate but specifically by a law to someone at any time, even to a private citizen,[63] with the power of inflicting capital punishment or of punishing criminals capitally.[64] Otherwise, it is defined as the power of preventing crime.[65] For some magistrates, by right of magistracy proper, taxes are collected as pure command.[66] Some authors disagree[67] and think that here the custom of each place ought to be considered. Elsewhere, this is called punishment,[68] or it is called a license for inflicting public discipline.[69]

27. Today There Is No Pure Command — Today, according to our customs, there is no example of pure command because, by a tacit right, vengeance and the power to inflict capital punishment follow a magistrate, and it is exercised by right of magistracy.[70] In this instance, a magistrate ought to look at the limits and purposes of each command: How long does it last? What is its extent? In what business does it apply? Does this command come from custom, a statute, or the concession of a superior?[71]

28. Why It Is Called Pure — Moreover, this command is called pure because by itself it is untainted, naked, alone, and separated from jurisdiction,[72] or because it exists in coercion alone, which is properly called command, not in ordinance or investigation, which is called jurisdiction. It is also called pure because this command is separate from a magistracy or from that power that is granted by right of magistracy, to which this pure command does not belong and with which it is not involved according to its own nature. With respect to mixed command, this is called pure command.[73] In fact, canon lawyers have called it sole command,[74] and the Greeks translated pure command as single command (μόνος). Thus, there are the terms pure rigidity, pure condition,[75] pure law of nations,[76] pure judicial procedure,[77] and pure punishment.[78] Therefore, a statute renders judgment in pure command, not a magistrate as in mixed command.[79]

29. The Different Terms for Pure Command — This pure command is also called supreme power, punishment,[80] the command of one who has greater power,[81] power through excellence,[82] power of the sword and the right of the sword,[83] the fullest jurisdiction,[84] and command.[85] The symbol and sign of this command is the sword.[86] In Rome, these symbols were the fasces, as can be seen in Dionysius of Halicarnasus and Livy. Others call pure command high jurisdiction[87] and think that it was called pure because it was removed from private use.

In addition, with regard to official public power, sometimes when it has been ordered in a certain way it is entrusted in particular circumstances without jurisdiction and coercion and without the power of prosecution to a private citizen by someone who has the right to concede and entrust this power.

There are two types of this: substitution and mutual agreement.[88]

30. Substitutionary Power — Substitution is when power is granted from the specific and truly public power of an official to a private citizen,[89] including those situations that do not require the investigation of the transferring magistrate himself.[90]

31. Authorized, Foreign, and Delegated Power — It is also called transferred jurisdiction[91] or foreign jurisdiction.[92]

32. What an Ordinary Authorization Is — When it is given by a prince or the public provincial power, this power is called particular and ordinary jurisdiction (not foreign),[93] which is regular, perpetual, and universal;[94] has been allotted by a public authority to someone;[95] is given by the exercise of an ordinary right; or is that by which the totality of business is entrusted to someone.[96] This is also called delegated jurisdiction[97] or command separated from its magistrate and naked.[98] In fact, the person to whom this jurisdiction is transferred is called the procurator, deputy, substitute, or agent, or even the trustee of an entrusting magistrate.[99] Donellus[100] calls him a magistrate without command and power,[101] who, by use and exercise is considered to have the place of a magistrate even though he is not so by office and power. Elsewhere he is called an appointed judge[102] who oversees the prosecution of lesser things[103] or a special judge[104] or a delegated judge.[105]

33. The Force of Authorized Jurisdiction — The force of authorized jurisdiction consists in him, because having it, he has sole power of investigating and judging,[106] not however of appointing and executing.[107] Therefore, he has sole power of investigation and judicial decision-making.[108]

34. This Cannot Be Transferred or Yielded — This power he cannot transfer or grant to another person.[109] This regulation is relaxed, so that, although he is unable to transfer it to another person, when an investigation of the case requires it, he can.[110]

35. Its Limit and Form — In the exercise and use of his granted jurisdiction, he follows the procedure prescribed to him and performs the duties of the one who is transferring it[111] and administers that person's jurisdiction[112] while possessing no individual jurisdiction of his own.[113] He does this in such a way that the execution of his decisions pertains to the transferred jurisdiction only.[114]

36. When It Is Called Returned — This transferred jurisdiction, once the will of the one who transfers it has come to an end, is considered returned.[115] Once returned, this jurisdiction is called not private but cumulative.[116]

37. It Is Not Possible That the Exercise of Authority Be Remitted or Abdicated — As for the naked use and exercise of command, a magistrate is able to grant and transfer it to another,[117] but he cannot renounce this command from himself.[118] This is because the command clings to the person and, therefore, cannot be fully yielded to another.[119] He should not be quick to transfer his jurisdiction,[120] and he will instead transfer from those things that by law he has as a magistrate—that is, those things that were obtained at one time by judicial decisions and lesser things,[121] not those things that by the law of the magistracy were entrusted to him by virtue of that office.[122] Donellus thought that extraordinary procedures involving honoraria were among those things that at one time these magistrates were able to transfer.[123]

38. What Cannot Be Authorized — However, it is not possible to transfer those things that do not pertain to one's own jurisdiction.[124] Here, I include those things that they do not have by the law of their own magistracies but specifically by a statute or institution.[125]

39. When It Is Authorized Cumulatively or Individually — However, jurisdiction is transferred and yielded to another person cumulatively, not privately or totally, when that person is not able to investigate and pronounce judgment alone but so that when he concedes this jurisdiction, he may retain the greater jurisdiction and be able to exercise it at the same time,[126] that is, unless a statute itself confers jurisdiction or the form of the concession is private and total and establishes distinct jurisdictions.[127] This has varied in different time periods.

40. Paurmeister's[128] Distinction — For, at one time, when jurisdiction was a part of state law and existed in the possession of the Roman state alone, its use was entrusted for a time both in ordinary and extraordinary circumstances to the magistrates alone. At that time, it was always possible for a higher magistrate who yields power to exercise this power along with the other magistrates because he still would retain it among all the temporal and entrusted magistracies who would exercise the entrusted jurisdiction not in their name but in the name of the one who yielded the power. This opinion is attributed to Bartolus.[129] According to the situation in our time, every jurisdiction is considered to have been granted not privately but cumulatively, whether it has been yielded by emperors, princes, the leading citizens of the Empire—whether by their inferiors, subjects, or individual people—or simply the entire population. In other words, this jurisdiction should be understood to be imparted at all times in such a way that the person who yields the jurisdiction does not renounce his entire jurisdiction or, at least for legal pronouncements, there still exist the right to appeal to the higher authority or other legal possibilities, so that not only might the one who yields jurisdiction not be considered a private citizen by the highest law but also that he might be able to work with those to whom the jurisdiction has been yielded by preparing the work for them, working together with them, or providing instruction.[130] As for use at this time, Paurmeister believes that there is a distinction between expressly yielded and tacitly yielded jurisdiction, between, on the one hand, a thing authorized universally or generally, and, on the other hand, singularly; or, on the one hand, a privilege bestowed perpetually, and, on the other hand, by designation of use-right, or by title of a fief, pledge, deed, or lease.

In any transferred jurisdiction or in a certain type of jurisdiction when the magistrates have been appointed or delegated, the old law that I mentioned above still holds. However, as long as those who have jurisdiction by right and have properly obtained it either by contract or by privilege—even if they are emperors, princes, nobles, imperial citizens, or nobles and citizens of a subject people, some being new nobles of the Empire by order of the Apostolic Camera,[131] others by tradition—we see a reason introduced against the old law. This is in order that, as far as first judicial proceedings, superiors might not fight with inferiors either by anticipating or going ahead of them, and so that jurisdiction would return to the superior not on its own, but by the action of claimants and lower judicial decisions, by appeal, of course, or by the denial or protraction of justice, or by the crime of negligence or suspicion of negligence.[132]

41. The Old Magistracies of the Romans — Long ago among the Romans, some magistracies were Roman, some were municipal, some were provincial. Some were ordinary magistracies of various rank; others were extraordinary. Ordinary magistracies of higher rank were senators, consuls, plebian tribunes, censors, and urban prefects. Lesser ordinary magistracies were state treasurers, plebian superintendents, curule superintendents, managers, leaders of the different tribes, triumvirs, quatuorvirs, quinquevirs, decemvirs, and the like. Extraordinary magistracies of higher rank included the regent, dictator, commander of the cavalry, centumviri, military tribunes, and the like. Lesser extraordinary magistracies were those who investigated high treason, quaestors investigating parricide or other capital offenses, the prefect in charge of the grain supply, those who regulated debts, the commissioners in charge of the fleet, the prefect of the fire brigade, and the like. Provincial magistracies included governors of provinces and administrators, such as praetor, quaestor, prefect, judge, proconsul, praetorian prefect, and the like.[133]

42. What the Power of Mutual Agreement Is — Mutual agreement is the power that is granted to a private citizen by private citizens who have no public power for the purpose of investigating and rendering a decision for their own disputed situation without jurisdiction and without the previous decision of a public power.[134] It is called arbitration because it does not happen against one's will but by the will, decision, and choice of both sides.[135]

Notes

1. *Geil. lib. 1. observ. 17. Fernand Vasqui. illust. controv. lib. 1. cap. 8. Mynsing. cent. 5. obs. 8.*

2. *vide Hieronym. de monte cap. 3. de finib. regund. Losaum de jure universit. part. 1. cap. 2. num. 7. 8. l. 6. §. qui universas. l. congrui. 13. de offic. praesid.*

3. *Bart. in l. unic. num. 5. Cod. de metrop. Beryt. lib. 11. Marcus decis 366. num. 13. 14. vol. 1. Losa. de jure univ. part. 1. c. 2. Hieronym. de monte de finib. reg. c. 4. num. 7.*

4. *tit. Cod. de rect. provinc. & toto fere lib. 1. C.*

5. *Geil. lib. 1. observ. 97. Boër. decis. 202. Heig. lib. 1. quaest. 2. Choppin. lib. 1. de doman. reg. tit. 6. num. 18. Paurmeist. lib. 2. c. 10. num. 7. 8. de jurisd. Matth. Stephani lib. 2. part. 1. c. 4 nu. 1. 2. & seqq. Pet. Gregor. Syntagm. jur. lib. 6. cap. 9.*

6. *Paurmeist. d. loc. Andr. Knich. de jure territorii cap. 4. Geil. lib. 1. observ. 21.*

7. *Wesenbec. consil. 27. nu. 28. Disentit Paurm. lib. 2. cap. ult. num. 18. de jurisd. vide in Polit. c. 18. Rosenthal de feud. cap. 2. quaest. 2. Geil. de arrest. cap. 6. num. 9. Matth. Steph. lib. 2. part. 1. cap. 6. de jurisd. Heig. d. loc. Pacian. lib. 2. c. 35. & seqq. de probat. Borch. de feud. cap. quae sunt regal.*

8. *Geil. lib. 1. cap. 6. num. 19. de pac. publica. & lib. 2. observat. 57. num. 7. 8. Wesenbec. consil. 40. num. 44. & consil. 27. num. 28. Donell. lib. 17. com. cap. 22.*

9. *l. deprecatio 9. ad L. Rhod. de jact. l. bene a Zenone. Cod. de quad. praescript. Wesenbec. consil. 97.*

10. *Rosenthal lib. 1. de feud. conclus. 10. & 13. cap. 5. Covarruv. pract. quaest. cap. 4. Roland. a Valle consil. 1. num. 138. vol. 2 & idem nu. 141. & seqq. consil. 1. vol. 2. Bossius de principe num. 92. & seqq. Matth. Stephani de jurisdict. lib. 2. part. 1. memb. 2. cap. 1.*

11. *Geil. lib. 1. obs. 17. Fern. Vasqui lib. 1. illust. controv. cap. 8. num. 17. & seqq. Boër. decis. 304.*

12. *l. 11. l. 12. l. 13. l. 19. l. 6. de offic. praesid. l. 7. l. 8. l. 9. de offic. procons. l. 6. solent. de offic. procons. Menoch. lib. 1. quaest. 12. num. 8. arb. judic. & quaest. 14. & 87. Genes. cap. 41. 40.41. & seqq. Deuter. cap. 1. Jerem. cap. 7. 31. cap. 31. 5. cap. 32. 35. 1. Regum. cap. 9. 22.23. Exod. cap. 18. 21. & seqq.*

13. *l. penult. de offic. praesid. l. 1. de offic. procurat. Caesar.*

14. *l. unic. de offic. praefect. praetor. l. 5. more de jurisdict.*

15. *l. 1. in pr. & §. 1. l. 2. l. 3. l. 4. de offic. ejus cui est mand. jurisd.*

16. *l. 6. & quia. de jurisdict. l. 1. de offic. praefect. August. l. penult. de offic. ejus cui est mand. jurisdict. Novell. 15.*

17. *l. 1. l. 2. de offic. ejus. l. penult. & ult. Cod. com. vel. epist. vicar. rei jud. non hab. lib. 7. tit. 57.*

18. *l. 6. de jurisdict.*

19. *l. unic. Cod. ut om. judic. tam civil. quam criminal. post depos. administr. Petrus Gregorius lib. 47. suntag. cap. 21. num. 3. 4. 5. Mynsing. cent. 5. observ. 8.*

20. *l. 1. l. 2. de jurisd. l. 1. l. ult. de offic. ejus cui est mand. jurisd.*

21. *l. 5. more. de jurisdict. l. 1. l. 3. de offic. ejus cui est mandat. jurisdict.*

22. *l. 1. l. 2. l. 3. 10. l. 11. de jurisdict. l. 1. si quis jus dic. non. obtemp. l. 58. de judic.*

23. *§. praetorum. Instit. de jur. nat. gent. & civil. Roman. cap. 13. 1. Pet. cap. 2. 13.14. 2. Chron. c. 20. 19.*

24. *l. 1. l. 2. l. 3. de jurisdict.*

25. *tot. tit. de jurisdict. Matth. Stephani lib. 1. c. 2. de jurisd.*

26. *l. 3. de jurisd.*

27. *argum. tit. de jurisd. l. 1. l. ult. de offic. ejus. l. 3. de offic. praesid. l. 1. de extraord. cognit. Stephan. de jurisd. lib. 1. c. 6.*

28. *l. 3. in fin. de postul. l. 16. §. 5 de minor. Robert. lib. 4. sent. cap. 22. Corasius lib. 22. miscell. cap. 17. num. 15. Alciatus lib. 2. parad. cap. 8. Cujac. lib. 2. ad Papin.*

29. *l. ult. de offic. ejus cui est.*

30. *Cujac. ad l. 1. in Papin. de offic. ejus cui est mand. jurisd.*

31. *Cujac. d. loc. Donell. lib. 17. com. c. 8.*

32. *l. 99. notionem. ubi. Goedd. de verb. signific. l. 5. de re jud.*

33. *l. 8. de transact. l. 11. §. 2. de jurisdict. d. l. 5. l. 1. de praetor. stipul.*

34. *l. pen. in fin. de just. & jur. l. 9. judices. Cod. de judic. Johan. cap. 7. 51. Deuter. cap. 17.*

35. *Auth. jubemus. Cod. de judic. l. 3. §. 1. de recept. arbit.*

36. *Duaren. in tit. de jurisd. per l. si idem. de jurisd. l. 1. de extr. cognit. Matth. Steph. lib. 1. c. 5. de jurisd.*

37. *l. 15. a Divo Pio. de re judic. l. 2. de jurisdict. l. ult. de officio ejus cui est mand. jurisdict.*

38. *d. l. ult. de offic. ejus cui est mand. Novell. 15. c. 1. 2. 3. 6.*

39. *d. l. ult. l. 14. de re jud. l. 4. de jurisdict. §. 1. 2. 3. Institut. de interdict. l. ult. ne quid in loc. publ. Donell. lib. 17. com. cap. 8.*

40. *l. 1. de aqua quotid. & aest. l. 14. de re judic. l. 1. de rivis.*

41. *l. 1. §. ult. l. ult. de offic. ejus cui est. mand. tit. quod quisque jur. in al. stat. l. 1. si quis jus dicent. non obtemp.*

42. *l. 58. judicium. de judic. l. 31. Divus. de sicar. l. 7. de jurisd. l. 11. de in jus vocand.*

43. *l. 4. de jurisd.*

44. *l. 13. congruit. de offic. praesid. Roman. cap. 13.*

45. *argum. l. 9. judices. l. 17. certi. Cod. de judic.*

46. *l. 2. §. ult. de jud. l. 2. si quis in jus vocat. l. 2. l. 3. Cod. de mod. mulct.*

47. *l. 12. de jurisdict. jussui non obtemperanti. l. 1. si quis jus dicent. non obtemp. l. ult. l. 1. §. ult. de offic. ejus, cui est mandat.*

48. *d. l. ult.*

49. *l. 58. judicium. de judic.*

50. *l. ea. quae 26. ad municip. l. 4. de jurisdict.*

51. *l. 11. respiciendum. de poen. Duaren in l. more. de jurisd. Clar. quaest. 8. pract. crim. §. fin. Marant. part. 4. dist. 1 num. 82.*

52. *l. 3. de jurisd. l. 1. §. ult. de offic. ejus cui est mand. jurisd. Menoch. lib. 1. arb. judic. cas. 74. num. 20.*

53. *d. l. 3. l. 4. de jurisdict. l. ea quae 26. ibi, magis imperii. ad municip.*

54. *Menoch. d. cas. 74. num. 20. 21.*

55. Ed. note: Matthias Stephani (d. 1646) was a legal scholar and professor at the University of Greifswald. Althusius cites Stephani's *Tractatus de jurisdictione* (1611) several times in this chapter.

56. *l. 1. §. ult. l. ult. de offic. ejus cui est mandat. l. 2. de jurisdict. l. ult. Cod. ubi & apud quem cogn.*

57. *d. l. ult. de offic. ejus. l. unic. si quis jus dicent. non. obtemp. l. 2. de jurisdict. Menoch. d. cas. 74. num. 20. 21.*

58. *ut explicat Donellus.*

59. *l. 3. l. 4. de jurisdict. l. 1. de offic. ejus. vid. Fachin. lib. 9. cap. 95. contr. illust.*

60. *d. l. 1. §. ult. l. 3. l. ult. de offic. ejus.*

61. *l. 3. etsi. de offic. ejus. l. 12. cum praetor. de judic.*

62. *d. l. 3. Cujac. lib. 21. observ. cap. 30. Duarenus lib. 1. disput. cap. 52. & in d. l. 3. de jurisdict. Donellus lib. 17. com. cap. 7. & cap. 8. Robert. lib. 4. sent. cap. 22. Dissentit Anton. Faber lib. 4. conject. cap. 4. Zasius in l. 3. de jurisdict. De exemplis mixti imperii, vid. Muscorn. de jurisdict. nu. 151. Longovall. in l. 3. de jurisdict. & Zasium in d. l. 3. Alciat. lib. 2. par. cap. 7. Pet. Gregor. lib. 47. cap. 21. num. 13. 14. syntag. Donell. d. lib. 17. cap. 8. Hotoman. lib. 7. obs. c. 16.*

63. *l. 2. §. exactis. de origin. jur. l. 6. solet. de offic. procons. l. 1. §. 1. l. 5. de offic. ejus cui est mand. jurisd. l. 1. ad L. Cornel. de sicar. l. 131. §. ult. de verbor. signifi. l. 7. de offic. proconsul.*

64. *l. 3. de jurisd. l. 3. l. 13. congruit. de offic. praesid. nemo. 70. de regul. Actor. cap. 26. 10. 11. 12. Francisc. de Claper. de jurisd. conclus. 4.*

65. *l. 1. Cod. qui non poss. ad libert. per ven. Cujac. lib. 1. quaest. Papin. & ad l. 1. de offic. ejus cui est mand. Donell. lib. 17. com. cap. 8. Hotoman. lib. 3. obs. cap. 4.*

66. *l. 1. de offic. ejus l. illicitas. §. qui universas. de offic. praesid. l. 6. solent. l. 5. de offic. procons. l. 1. §. 1. de poen. Donell. d. cap. 8. vid. Covarruv. lib. 3. var. resolut. cap. ult. Menoch. lib. 1. arb. quaest. 54. num. 9. cas. 74. num. 44. 45. Clar. quaest. 41. §. fin. nu. 4.*

67. *Muscornus num. 135. de jurisdict. Walter lib. 2. miscell. cap. 9. Pet. Gregor. lib. 47. syntag. cap. 21. num. 20. 21.*

68. *l. 1. §. pen. de offic. ejus, cui est mand.*

69. *l. unic. de offic. praefect. praetor.*

70. *Donell. d. lib. 17. com. cap. 8. Francisc. de Claper. de jurisdict. conclus. 2. num. 8. Cujac. d. loc. Pet. Gregor. d. loc.*

71. *Pet. Gregor. d. loc. argum. l. 1. Cod. de. emancip. lib. l. 1. Cod. quand. Imp. Novell. 15. c. 2. & seqq. l. 1. de offic. ejus. l. 1. ad L. Jul. de amb.*

72. *argum. l. 62. in fin. de jur. dot. l. 27. de donat.*

73. *Donell. lib. 17. com. cap. 8. Duaren. de jurisdict. cap. 3. & in l. 3. Vacon. a Vacun. lib. 6. declarat. cap. 2. num. 7.*

74. *l. 5. de verb. oblig.*

75. *l. cum servus. de cond. & demonst.*

76. *l. 31. de poss.*

77. *l. qui res. §. mihi. de solut. l. 5. stipulatio. de verb. obl.*

78. *l. 1. in fin. si quis jus dic. non obtemp. Dissentit Alciat. in l. 215. de verb. sign.*

79. *l. 15. ordine. ad municip. l. 1. ad SC. Turpill.*

80. *l. 5. C. de jurisd. l. 13. de offic. praesid. l. 1. §. ult. de offic.*

81. *l. si quod. de off. procons.*

82. *l. 3. de jurisd.*

83. *l. 6. de offic. procons. l. 6. §. 8. de offic. praesid. l. 71. nemo. de reg. jur.*

84. *l. 7. si in. §. 2. de offic. procons.*

85. *l. 2. de in jus vocand.*

86. *Suet. in Vitell. c. 8. Josu. c. 5. 13.14. Job. c. 19. 1. Sam. c. 15. 13. Exod. cap. 18. 4. c. 22. 24. Deut. c. 13. 15. c. 20. 13.16. c. 32. 41.42.*

87. *Bartol. Alciat. Zas. & Jas. in l. 3. de jurisd.*

88. *tit. C. de offic. ejus qui vicem alter. gerit. tit. de offic. ejus cui est mand. jurisd. tit. de recept. arb.*

89. *l. more 5. l. 16. l. 17 de jurisdict. l. 1. l. 2. l. 3. de offic. ejus cui est mand. jurisd. tit. C. de off. ejus qui vicem alt gerit.*

90. *l. 2. C. de pedan. judic.*

91. *l. 1. §. 1. l. 2. l. 5. de off. ejus cui est mand. jurisd. l. 5. more. de jurisd.*

92. *d. l. 1. §. 1. l. 3. etsi de off. ejus cui est mand. jurisd.*

93. *l. ult. C. ubi senat. vel clariss. l. 1. de const. pr. l. 1. ad L. Jul. de amb. Novell. 15. c. 3. Luc. c. 10. 16. 1. Pet. c. 2. 14.*

94. *Paurmeist. lib. 1. c. 10. n. 28. de jurisd.*

95. *d. c. 10.*

96. *vide Menoch. lib. 2. praes. 16. vide infra lib. 3. c. 4.*

97. *l. 2. C. de dilat. l. 5. cum auth. seq. l. 16. C. de judic.*

98. *l. 5. l. 15. ubi gl. Bart. & Duar. de re judicat. l. a judice 5. C. de judic. l. cognitionum. de var. & extraord. cognit.*

99. *l. 1. §. 1. l. 2. l. 3. l. 6. de off. ejus cui est mand. jurisd. Duar. de jurisd. c. 7. c. 8. Donell. lib. 17. c. 8. comment.*

100. Ed. note: Hugo Donellus (1527–1591), or Hugues Doneau, was a French legal scholar who taught at the University of Heidelberg, the University of Leiden, and ultimately concluded his career at the University of Altdorf.

101. *l. 32. nec. de jur.*

102. *l. 2. 3. 4. 5. C. de pedan jud. l. ult. C. ubi & apud quos. l. 4. praetor. de tut. & curat. l. 38. de poenis.*

103. *l. 2. l. ult. C. de peda. jud. Novell. 82. ubi Cujac.*

104. *l. fin. de offic. praetor. l. 5. de offic. praesid.*

105. *tit. C. qui pro sua jurisd. judic. dar. poss. tit. de offic. delgat. extr.*

106. *l. a Divo 15. ubi Duaren. de re judic. l. properandum. §. fin autem. C. de re judic. Menoch. lib. 1. arbitr. judic. quaest. 74. num. 3. Donell. lib. 17. comm. cap. 6. a se ipso dissentiens lib. 17. cap. 23.*

107. *d. l. 15. a Divo Pio. d. l. properandum. §. fin. autem. Dissentit Donell. d. loco.*

108. *l. 5. ait. l. 15 a Divo. de re judic. l. 99. notionem. de verb. sign. l. penult. l. de quare. de judic. l. 8. de transact. l. ult. C. ubi & apud quem in integr. restit. l. cognitionum. de var. & extraordin. cognitio.*

109. *l. 6. & quia. de jurisdict. tit. C. de offic. ejus qui vic. arg. §. penult. ult. Instit. de usufruct. l. nemo plus. de regulis juris. Donellus d. c. 8. Menoch. lib. 1. arb. jud. quaest. 54. & 74. num. 45. & seqq.*

110. *per l. solet. de offic. procons. Novell. 134. c. 1. 2. 3. 4. Novell. 15. & 128. c. 19. c. 20. vide Menoch. quaest. 2. d. lib. 1. arbitr. judic.*

111. *l. 16. l. 17. de jurisdict.*

112. *l. 1. §. 1. de offic. ejus cui est mandat.*

113. *l. 1. §. 1. l. 3. de offic. ejus.*

114. *Zas. late in l. 5. de jurisd. Hart. ab Epping. lib. 2. obs. 15. 17. tit. 15. Marant. part. 4. dist. 5. Menoch. lib. 1. arb. quaest. 54. & 74.*

115. *vide Menoch. lib. 1. quaest. 79. 68. Covarruv. variar. resolut. lib. 3. cap. 5.*

116. *Myns. cent. 6. obs. 99. Menoch. lib. 2. praes. 18. num. 31. 32. Paurmeist. lib. 1. c. 29. de jurisd.*

117. *l. pen. de offic. praesid. l. cui muneris. de mun. & honor. atque l. 16. solet. l. 17. l. 5. l. 6. de jurisd. l. 1. de offic. ejus.*

118. *d. l. pen. de off. praesid.*

119. *d. l. pen.*

120. *l. 2. C. de pedan. judic.*

121. *l. 2. l. ult. C. de pedan. judic.*

122. *Donellus late lib. 17. comm. cap. 22. argum. Novell. 60. §. illud. Authent. ad haec. C. de judic.*

123. *l. 1. de extraord. cogn. De quibus videre licet in l. quod si. §. ult. de minor. l. 3. §. 1. de lib. exhib. l. 1. §. 1. de rei vind. l. pecunia. §. actionis. de verb. sign. l. solent de offic. procons. l. 1 de offic. ejus. l. nec quicquam. §. ubi de offi. procons. l. 2. C. de assessor. vide Menoch. lib. 1. quaest. 2. arb. judic.*

124. *tit. C. qui pro sua jurisd. jud. dar. poss. l. 4. §. ult. de off. procons.*

125. *l. 1. de off. ejus cui est mand. l. cum hi 7. §. sed nos. de transact. l. penult. l. 12. §. 1. l. 80. de judic. l. 2. C. de pedan. jud. Novell. 15.*

126. *Menoch. lib. 2. praesumpt. 18. & lib. 1. quaest. 40. arb. jud. & quaest. 74. Myns. cent. 6. obs. 99. per l. 1. C. de defens. civit. Novell. 15. c. 3.*

127. *Menoch. d. lib. 2. praesumpt. 18. & lib. 1. arbit. quaest. 40. Covarr. pract. quaest. c. 1. c. 2. late. Paurmeist. lib. 1. cap. 29. de jurisdict.*

128. Ed. note: Tobias Paurmeister (1553–1616) was a German legal and political scholar. Althusius interacts with Paurmeister's *Jurisdictione Imperii Romani* (1608).

129. Ed. note: Bartolus de Saxoferrato (1313–1357) was an Italian legal scholar and one of the most influential jurists of late medieval Europe.

130. *Menoch. lib. 2. praes. 17.*

131. *Constit. part. 2. tit. 1.* Ed. note: The Apostolic Camera was the administrative body with responsibility over papal territories and financial affairs from the twelfth century to the nineteenth century.

132. *Paurmeist. d. loc. per alleg. ibid.*

133. *de quibus omnibus & singulis consulendus Johan. Rofinus lib. 7. antiqui. Roman. & Praevot. de magist. Roman. c. 4. & tit. 9. de Senator. tit. de officio consul. & seqq. libri primi. D. & tit. C. de offic. praefect. praetor. tit. C. de offic. praefect. praetor. Africa. tit. seqq. usque ad finem libri primi Codicis.*

134. *tot. tit. de recept. arb. Geil. lib. 1. obs. 40. per l. privatorum. C. de jurisd.*

135. *l. 1. de recept. arb. l. 14. l. 18. de jurisdict. vide lib. 3. cap. 4. Hujus loci est tit. D. & C. de jurisd. de offic. ejus cui est mand. jurisd. tit. si quis jus dicenti non obtemp. tit. de offic. consul. & seqq. usque ad finem. lib. 1. D. & tit. C. de offic. praefect. praetor. & seqq. usque ad finem. lib. 1. C. tit. C. de offic. ejus qui vices alter. gerit. tit. D. de recept. arbit. tit. C. de pedan. judic.*

About the Contributors

Jordan J. Ballor (Dr. theol., University of Zurich) is a research fellow at the Acton Institute for the Study of Religion & Liberty and serves as executive editor of the *Journal of Markets & Morality*. He is also the author of *Covenant, Causality, and Law: A Study in the Theology of Wolfgang Musculus* (Vandenhoeck & Ruprecht, 2012) and *Ecumenical Babel: Confusing Economic Ideology and the Church's Social Witness* (Christian's Library Press, 2010).

Stephen J. Grabill (PhD, Calvin Theological Seminary) serves as senior research scholar in theology and director of programs at the Acton Institute for the Study of Religion & Liberty. He is editor emeritus of the *Journal of Markets & Morality*, as well as author of *Rediscovering the Natural Law in Reformed Theological Ethics* (Eerdmans, 2006) and editor of *Sourcebook in Late-Scholastic Monetary Theory* (Lexington, 2007).

Jeff Veenstra (MA History, Pennsylvania State University) is Dean of Faculty and Instruction at Tempe Preparatory Academy, a Great Books school, in Tempe, Arizona, where he teaches advanced Latin, Greek, and Humanities. He has also taught at Calvin College, Hope College, Grand Valley State University, and Pennsylvania State University. In addition, he produced translations for the *Journal of Markets & Morality* as well as presented papers at various conferences on early Christian apocalyptic thought.

John Witte, Jr. (JD, Harvard Law School) is Director of the Center for the Study of Law and Religion, Jonas Robitscher Professor of Law, and Alonzo L. McDonald Family Foundation Distinguished Professor at Emory University. A specialist in legal history, marriage law, and religious liberty, he has published two hundred articles, fifteen journal symposia, and twenty-seven books.

Christian's LIBRARY PRESS

Founded in 1979 by Gerard Berghoef and Lester DeKoster, **Christian's Library Press** has been committed to publishing influential texts on church leadership, the vocation of work, and stewardship for more than thirty years. During that time Berghoef and DeKoster wrote significant works including *The Deacons Handbook*, *The Elders Handbook*, and *God's Yardstick*, which still are in demand today. After the passing of Lester DeKoster in 2009, the imprint is now administered by the Acton Institute for the Study of Religion & Liberty. For more information about Christian's Library Press, visit www.clpress.com.

ACTON INSTITUTE

With its commitment to pursue a society that is free and virtuous, the **Acton Institute for the Study of Religion & Liberty** is a leading voice in the international environmental and social policy debate. With offices in Grand Rapids, Michigan, and Rome, Italy, as well as affiliates in four other nations around the world, the Acton Institute is uniquely positioned to comment on the sound economic and moral foundations necessary to sustain humane environmental and social policies. The Acton Institute is a nonprofit, ecumenical think tank working internationally to "promote a free and virtuous society characterized by individual liberty and sustained by religious principles." For more on the Acton Institute, please visit www.acton.org.

Sources in Early Modern Economics, Ethics, and Law

Jordan J. Ballor and Stephen J. Grabill, General Editors

Books in This Series

A Treatise on the Alteration of Money
Juan de Mariana
Translated by Patrick T. Brannan • Annotations by Stephen J. Grabill
Introduction by Alejandro A. Chafuen

On the Law in General
Girolamo Zanchi
Translated by Jeffrey J. Veenstra • Introduction by Stephen J. Grabill

On Law and Power
Johannes Althusius
Translated by Jeffrey J. Veenstra • Introductions by Stephen J. Grabill
and John Witte Jr.

On Exchange and Usury
Thomas Cajetan
Translated by Patrick T. Brannan • Introduction by Raymond de Roover

On Righteousness, Oaths, and Usury
Wolfgang Musculus
Translated by Todd M. Rester • Introduction by Jordan J. Ballor

On Exchange
Martín de Azpilcueta
Translated by Jeannine Emery • Introduction by Rodrigo Muñoz

A Treatise on Money
Luis de Molina
Translated by Jeannine Emery • Introduction by Rudolf Schuessler

The Mosaic Polity
Franciscus Junius
Translated by Todd M. Rester • Edited by Andrew M. McGinnis

Of the Law of Nature
Matthew Hale
Edited by David S. Sytsma

On Sale, Securities, and Insurance
Leonardus Lessius
Translated by Wim Decock and Nicholas De Sutter • Introduction by Wim Decock

Made in United States
Orlando, FL
10 November 2026

90498869R10079